The Social Justice
Bible Challenge

A 40 Day Bible Challenge

D1512584

This collection © 2017 Marek P. Zabriskie

Second printing, 2018.

Individual essays are the property of the authors.

All rights reserved.

ISBN: 978-0-88028-450-9

Printed in USA

Forward Movement
inspire disciples. empower evangelists.

The Social Justice Bible Challenge

A 40 Day Bible Challenge

Edited by Marek P. Zabriskie

FORWARD MOVEMENT
Cincinnati, Ohio

To my parents, Charles and Gail Zabriskie, who taught me the importance of caring for others, especially those in need

Preface

The Bible Challenge began as a simple idea: to encourage daily reading of scripture. Simple ideas can bring forth great change.

Developing a daily spiritual discipline or practice is crucial for all Christians who wish to be faithful followers of Jesus. Saint Augustine and many other great Christians have written about the power of reading the Bible quietly on our own. There is no other book in the world that can so transform the human heart, motivate the human spirit, and give us the mind that was in Christ Jesus himself.

The Bible remains the world's best-selling book year after year. However, Episcopalians, Roman Catholics, and other mainline Christians often do not read it. Church historian and author Diana Butler Bass reports that among the 22,000 Christian groups and denominations in the United States, Episcopalians are the best-educated group but drop to nearly last when it comes to biblical literacy.

The goal of The Bible Challenge is to help individuals develop a lifelong, daily spiritual discipline of reading the Bible so that their lives may be constantly transformed and renewed. Studies reveal that prayerfully engaging scripture is the best way for Christians to grow in their faith and love of Jesus.

More than 500,000 persons in 2,500 churches in over fifty countries are now participating in The Bible Challenge. We also offer The Bible Challenge Gospel Series: reading each book (Matthew, Mark, Luke, and John) over a 50-day period. *The Social Justice Bible Challenge* builds upon this hunger to engage in scripture and connects our desire to help with God's mandate to love and serve others. These Bible Challenge books are an ideal resource for individuals, churches, and dioceses during Lent, Easter, or any time of the year.

Regular engagement with the Bible develops a strong Christian faith, enhances our experience of worship, and helps to create a more committed, articulate, and contagious Christian. This is exactly what the world needs today.

With prayers and blessings for your faithful Bible reading,

The Rev. Marek P. Zabriskie
Founder of The Bible Challenge
Director of the Center for Biblical Studies
www.thecenterforbiblicalstudies.org
Rector of St. Thomas' Episcopal Church
Fort Washington, Pennsylvania

How to Read the Bible Prayerfully

Welcome to The Social Justice Bible Challenge. We are delighted that you are interested in reading God's life-transforming Word. It will change and enrich your life. Here are some suggestions to consider as you get started:

- You can begin The Social Justice Bible Challenge at any time of year.

- Each day has a manageable amount of reading, a meditation, a few questions, and a prayer, written by a host of wonderful authors.

- We suggest that you try to read the Bible each day. This is a great spiritual discipline to establish.

- If you need more than forty days to read through *The Social Justice Bible Challenge*, we support you in moving at the pace that works best for you. And if you want to keep going when you're done, a list of additional scripture citations is included in the book of the back. Keep reading!

- Many Bible Challenge participants read the Bible using their iPad, iPhone, Kindle, or Nook, or listen to the Bible on CDs or on a mobile device using Audio.com, faithcomesthroughhearing.org, or Pandora radio. Find what works for you.

- Other resources for learning more about the Bible and engaging scripture can be found on our website, ForwardMovement.org. In addition, you can find a list of resources at thecenterforbiblicalresources.org. The center also offers a Read the Bible in a Year program and reading plans for the New Testament, Psalms, and Proverbs.

- Because the Bible is not a newspaper, it is best to read it with a reverent spirit. We advocate a devotional approach to reading the Bible, rather than reading it as a purely intellectual or academic exercise.

- Before reading the Bible, take a moment of silence to put yourself in the presence of God. We then invite you to read this prayer written by Archbishop Thomas Cranmer.

  Blessed Lord, who has caused all holy scriptures to be written for our learning: Grant us to hear them, read, mark, learn, and inwardly digest them, that we may embrace and ever hold fast the blessed hope of everlasting life, which you have given us in our Savior Jesus Christ; who lives and reigns with you and the Holy Spirit, one God, for ever and ever. Amen.

- Consider using the ancient monastic practice of *lectio divina*. In this form of Bible reading, you read the text and then meditate on a portion of it—be it a verse or two or even a single word. Mull over the words and their meaning. Then offer a prayer to God based on what you have read, how it has made you feel, or what it has caused you to ponder. Listen in silence for God to respond to your prayer.

- We encourage you to read in the morning, if possible, so that your prayerful reading may spiritually enliven the rest of your day. If you cannot read in the morning, read when you can later in the day. Try to carve out a regular time for your daily reading.

- One way to hold yourself accountable to reading God's Word is to form a group within your church or community—particularly any outreach and ministry groups. By participating in The Social Justice Bible

Challenge together, you can support one another in your reading, discuss the Bible passages, ask questions, and share how God's Word is transforming your life.

- Ask to have a notice printed in your church newsletter that you are starting a group to participate in The Social Justice Bible Challenge. Invite others to join you and to gather regularly to discuss the readings, ask questions, and share how they are transforming your life. Visit the Center for Biblical Resources website to see more suggestions about how churches can participate in The Bible Challenge.

- Have fun and find spiritual peace and the joy that God desires for you in your daily reading. The goal of the Center for Biblical Studies is to help you discover God's wisdom and to create a lifelong spiritual practice of daily Bible reading so that God may guide you through each day of your life.

- Once you've finished one complete reading of the Bible, start over and do it again. God may speak differently to you in each reading. Follow the example of U.S. President John Adams, who read through the Bible each year during his adult life. We highly advocate this practice.

- After participating in The Social Justice Bible Challenge, you will be more equipped to support and mentor others in reading the Bible—and to connect your ministry of advocacy and assistance with Holy Scripture.

We are thrilled that you are participating in The Bible Challenge. May God richly bless you as you prayerfully engage the scriptures each day. To learn more about The Bible Challenge, visit us at: www.thecenterforblicalstudies.org to see all of our resources.

The Social Justice Bible Challenge

A 40 Day Bible Challenge

Introduction

A decent provision for the poor is the true test of civilization.
—SAMUEL JOHNSON

The degree of civilization in a society
can be judged by entering its prisons.
—FYODOR DOSTOYEVSKY

A nation's greatness is measured by how it treats its weakest members.
—MAHATMA GANDHI

The test of morality of a society is what it does for its children.
—DIETRICH BONHOEFFER

…for the test of a civilization is the way that it cares
for its helpless members.
—PEARL S. BUCK

What kind of Christian are you? Do you, like many conservative evangelicals, focus on personal salvation? Or does social justice and outreach guide you as it does many members of liberal mainline churches?

Of course, the question itself sets up a false dichotomy. Neither practice should be pursued to the exclusion of the other. To be faithful followers of Christ is to dive deeply into scripture and prayer, seeking and receiving personal salvation. And to be faithful followers of Christ requires us to love our neighbor and to strike down injustices.

To weigh one more heavily than the other throws the gospel out of balance. That conservative evangelical churches and liberal mainline churches have struggled to find a balance between personal salvation and community redemption/restoration seems obvious.

This volume is an attempt to bridge the gap between the Bible and social justice. It highlights some of the Bible's most emphatic and powerful verses that command us to exercise compassion, treat everyone equally, and care for widows, orphans, strangers, and the poor. For those who are invested in the work of social justice, this book connects their compassion to God's Word. And for those who are deeply engaged in scripture, it commands action.

Broadly speaking, many denominations fail in this regard. For instance, my denomination, the Episcopal Church, excels at helping others in need, combatting poverty, and speaking out on issues of social justice. We tend to be more comfortable with outreach and mission than the interior work of studying the Bible and evangelizing. Perhaps your congregation or denomination is just the opposite: deeply rooted in scripture and comfortable with sharing a personal story of salvation but not connecting that to work in the world beyond the church doors.

Both groups face a similar problem: the critical combination of both knowing God's word and putting it into action.

The Bible has inspired Christians to found hospices, which have become hospitals that have healed the sick and hurting the world over. Christians have founded schools that have evolved into great universities. For centuries, monasteries functioned as academies of learning, homeless shelters, food distribution centers, and hospitals for entire communities. Today, individuals and denominations are on the front lines, advocating for refugees, appealing for equality for all people, regardless of race, age, or sexual orientation, and working tirelessly to help the poor, the homeless, the imprisoned, and the hungry.

To follow God's teaching on social justice means to stand up and demand that police in our communities and across our nation treat all citizens with the same respect and courtesy, not showing favoritism to whites over blacks, but providing equal service and protection for all. It calls us to demand that banks lend equally, giving some of our nation's poorest citizens in the most challenged neighborhoods the ability to borrow money and create and grow businesses.

Bono, the frontman of the Irish rock group U2 and outspoken philanthropist, addressed this issue at the 2006 National Prayer Breakfast in Washington, D.C. "It's no coincidence," he said, "that in the scriptures, poverty is mentioned more than 2,100 times. It's not an accident. That's a lot of airtime, 2,100 mentions. You know, the only time Christ is judgmental is on the subject of the poor. 'As you have done it unto the least of these my brethren, you have done it unto me' (Matthew 25:40)."

Bono is right; 2,100 mentions is a lot of airtime for poverty, especially when you realize that sin is only mentioned 1,610 times, and terms related to sex and sexuality are mentioned a mere 26 times. Yet, over the past few decades Christians have had passionate fights and divisive debates over a handful of texts about human sexuality. Meanwhile, little has been said about the 2,100 passages that demand our care for the poor and marginalized.

If we were to cut out all of the passages of scripture that speak about human sexuality, the Bible would remain almost completely intact. If, however, we were to remove all of the passages where God calls for justice and demands care for the poor, the resulting Bible would be substantively gutted, with sizeable gaps found on most pages. God cares passionately about poverty and justice—the evidence is on virtually every single page in the Bible.

In his best-selling book *The Purpose Driven Life*, author Rick Warren asks of evangelicals, "How can we have missed it?" Indeed, Christian evangelicals in the United States have been latecomers to recognizing the Bible's overwhelming message of compassion toward the poor and marginalized and the resounding call for Christians to address these groups. For decades, evangelicals have focused on "saving souls" and preaching about individual salvation. Today, more and more evangelical churches are discovering God's vital call to serve the neediest among us. Verna Dozier, a wonderful educator, theologian, and lay Episcopal leader in Washington, D.C., spoke about this disconnect in her book *The Dream of God*: "I believe the Christian church has distorted the call, narrowed it from a call to transform the world to a call to save the souls of individuals who hear and heed a specific message, narrowed it from a present possibility to a future fulfillment."

For Episcopalians, the call to combat poverty and address social injustices is embodied in the vows we take as our Baptismal Covenant:

Q: Will you seek and serve Christ in all persons, loving your neighbor as yourself?

A: *I will, with God's help.*

Q: Will you strive for justice and peace among all people, and respect the dignity of every human being?

A: *I will, with God's help.* (*The Book of Common Prayer*, p. 305)

Despite the fact that we also commit to "proclaim by word and example the Good News of God in Christ," we often prefer to preach through our actions rather than through our words. As a result, many of our members are passionate about outreach, mission trips, helping those in need, reducing poverty, and addressing social injustices, yet these same members often struggle to know where in the Bible God urges us to carry out this work. Micah 6:8 presents us with a very clear charge:

> [God] has told you, O mortal, what is good;
> and what does the Lord require of you
> but to do justice, and to love kindness,
> and to walk humbly with your God?

This is one of the most succinct and vital passages in the Bible. It summarizes what God would have us do. It is a verse worthy of committing to memory, writing down, and setting daily before our eyes. The Hebrew word for justice is *mishpat*, a word that puts an emphasis on action. The word for kindness used here is taken from the Hebrew word *chesedh*, which conveys God's unconditional and steadfast love, grace, and compassion. Chesedh supplies the motive or attitude that we carry within us, while mishpat is the resulting action of a heart ready to serve God by caring for those around us with justice, especially caring for the most vulnerable. Additionally, the Hebrew word that translates most closely to humble or righteous is *tzadeqah*, which means to lead a life with right relationships, not only with God but with everyone in our lives.

At the heart of social justice in the Bible is the notion of righteousness or living in a right relationship with God and with others. The biblical concept of tzadeqah calls us to examine each relationship and all of our conduct, ensuring that we act at all times with fairness and equity in our daily transactions. If tzadeqah were a reality, there would be no need to speak about social injustice or to combat poverty, because neither would exist. This book would be unnecessary. But since the time when the first scriptures were written, the poor have suffered and injustice has thrived. Still there are beacons of hope, examples of people living into the gospel call, modeling the type of care and love of the other that we might adopt in our own lives.

Throughout the Old Testament, there is a constant emphasis on caring for widows, orphans, strangers, foreigners, refugees, immigrants, and the poor. In Zechariah 7:9-10 we read:

> Thus says the LORD of hosts: Render true judgments,
> show kindness and mercy to one another; do not oppress
> the widow, the orphan, the alien, or the poor; and do not
> devise evil in your hearts against one another.

In the agrarian society that shaped the scholars who compiled the Hebrew scriptures, widows, orphans, immigrants, and the poor lacked power and status. They were the untouchable class of their day. Starvation, abuse, and exploitation were daily threats and familiar realities. The Bible makes it clear that we are—and will be—judged on how we treat the least among us. God cares passionately and relentlessly for those who face the greatest challenges in this life.

In the Sermon on the Mount, we read that Jesus goes up the mountain and sits down, which is what rabbis did when they offered their most profound teaching. He teaches them saying, "Blessed are the poor in spirit" (Matthew 5:3). In Luke's Gospel, Jesus gives a similar address, but he walks down to where the people were gathered and stands among them and says, "Blessed are you who are poor." (Luke 6:20) In Luke, Jesus does not say "poor in spirit," but simply "blessed are you who are *poor*." The Greek word is *ptokos*, which means the poorest of the poor. These are the people who are unsure on a daily basis whether they can feed their family and sustain their lives. Their plight touches God's heart, and in their lives God's presence is found.

Wander into any mainline Christian church and attend a class on basic Christianity, and you may find lessons focusing on Christian doctrines about heaven, hell, baptism, Communion, the nature of God, sin, redemption, salvation, sexuality, ethics, and grace. But perhaps a more truthful course on the basic tenets of Christianity would teach participants (disciples of Jesus) how to minister to the poor, the sick, the elderly, and those in prison, as well as advocacy measures for those without access to institutional power, basic or higher education, voice, or hope. Both methods of formation and education are needed, but teaching about Christian practices, behaviors, compassion, and responsibilities is just as vital as the teaching of Christian doctrine. The authentic preaching of the gospel requires both belief and practice.

Indeed, Jesus began his ministry with a mandate to care for the poor. In Luke 4:17-19, we read that Jesus went to the synagogue on the sabbath as was his custom and had them unroll the scrolls until they found a passage from the book of Isaiah:

> He unrolled the scroll and found the place
> where it was written:
>> "The Spirit of the Lord is upon me,
>> because he has anointed me
>> to bring good news to the poor.
>> He has sent me to proclaim release to the captives
>> and recovery of sight to the blind,
>> to let the oppressed go free,
>> to proclaim the year of the Lord's favor."

This was Jesus' mission statement—the opening proclamation of his ministry. Of all the texts that Jesus could have read aloud to the congregation, he selected one of the most powerful passages in the Hebrew scriptures to call our attention to the plight of those who suffer.

Jesus knew what it was like to be poor. He was born into a poor family. The gospels note that Jesus' parents offered two turtle doves as payment for Mary's rite of purification following Jesus' birth. The temple had a sliding scale for this ritual. Two turtle doves was the fee for the poor.

Jesus' mother, Mary, traveled from Nazareth to a Judean hill town in order to visit her cousin, Elizabeth, who was pregnant with John the Baptist. Upon greeting her cousin, Mary offered a song of praise that has gone down in history:

> My soul magnifies the Lord,
> and my spirit rejoices in God my Savior,
> for he has looked with favor on the lowliness of his servant.
> Surely, from now on all generations will call me blessed;
> for the Mighty One has done great things for me,
> and holy is his name.
> His mercy is for those who fear him
> from generation to generation.
> He has shown strength with his arm;
> he has scattered the proud in the thoughts of their hearts.
> He has brought down the powerful from their thrones,
> and lifted up the lowly;
> he has filled the hungry with good things,
> and sent the rich away empty (Luke 1:46b-53).

This is a revolutionary hymn sung by a teenage Jewish peasant, living in Roman-occupied Palestine, who is envisioning a world turned upside down—where the poor and downtrodden, those crushed by oppression, exploitation, and unfair conditions end up victorious—obtaining freedom and power. What must it have been like for Jesus to be raised by a mother who spoke openly against social injustices and called for eliminating the poverty that plagued her community? No doubt, her concern for social justice shaped Jesus' outlook on life. Story after story reinforces Jesus' compassion for the poor and for victims of injustice, living in poverty. Jesus raises the son of a poor widow (Matthew 9:13). He shows great respect to a woman who is a social outcast (Luke 7:38), and he speaks with women in public, something other men would never do (John 4:27).

Jesus constantly pushes against the boundaries of his society, stretching them to allow more people to be embraced by God's compassion, grace, and forgiveness. Jesus not only challenges his disciples to care for the poor and marginalized, he commands them to open their homes to the poor, the blind, the maimed, and the outcast. In Luke's Gospel we read:

> [Jesus] said also to the one who had invited him, "When you give a luncheon or a dinner, do not invite your friends or your brothers or your relatives or rich neighbors, in case they may invite you in return, and you would be repaid. But when you give a banquet, invite the poor, the crippled, the lame, and the blind. And you will be blessed, because they cannot repay you, for you will be repaid at the resurrection of the righteous" (Luke 12-14).

The early church appointed deacons to work with the poor and needy in the community. Deacons were to care for widows and orphans and to champion those who were most vulnerable in society. They helped with the daily distribution of food. While Christians were a tiny percentage of those living under the Roman occupation, they did remarkable acts of service for the poor. Many Romans admired them. Even the Christians' greatest opponents took note and said, "Look how they love one another."

Throughout the history of the church, saintly figures have offered gripping examples of care for the poor and the needy. Saint Francis of Assisi, the son of a wealthy cloth merchant, gave up his wealth in order to be one with the poor and to better serve those in need. Jonathan Edwards (1703-1758) was a fire-and-brimstone preacher, who started the spiritual renewal of the Great Awakening in the Americas. Yet, in his discourse "The Duty of Charity to the Poor," Edwards reveals a far more compassionate side: "Where have we any command in the Bible laid down in stronger terms, and in a more preemptory urgent manner, than the command of giving to the poor." Frederick Denison Maurice (1805-1872) helped to found the discipline of Christian Socialism, believing that capitalism appealed to selfishness and was not ideally suited to establishing the kingdom of God that Jesus envisioned. He suggested that the kingdom of God was not a future goal but rather a present reality. His writings and teachings inspired others to found urban churches to serve the poor.

Few have done more to care for the poor and fight for social justice than Archbishop Desmond Tutu. Widely credited with helping to dismantle apartheid in South Africa, Tutu once said, "If you are neutral in situations of injustice, you have chosen the side of the oppressor. If an elephant has its foot on the tail of a mouse, and you say that you are neutral, the mouse will not appreciate your neutrality." In this same vein, Pope Francis' huge heart for the poor has resulted in his preaching that God's other name is compassion. The Episcopal Church's Presiding Bishop, Michael Curry, blends a powerful faith rooted in the Bible and in prayer with a call to liberation and social justice. He has said:

> Jesus didn't start an institution, he started a movement.
> The same movement as Abraham and Sarah. The same
> movement as Moses and the Israelites. The same movement

Amos described, when he said, "Let justice roll down like a river, and righteousness like an ever flowing stream." This is a movement commissioned and commanded by God to transform this world from the nightmare we've too often made it, and into the dream that God has intended all along.

Following the footsteps of Jesus, alongside exceptional leaders like Pope Francis and Bishop Curry, we can blend a passion for the Bible and fervent prayer with a strong call for social justice and combating poverty. The poor are on God's heart and should be on ours. We are called to fight poverty and injustice wherever we find it and to support the millions of people around the world living in desperation.

Marek P. Zabriskie

Genesis 2:7-17

[7]Then the LORD God formed man from the dust of the ground, and breathed into his nostrils the breath of life; and the man became a living being. [8]And the LORD God planted a garden in Eden, in the east; and there he put the man whom he had formed. [9]Out of the ground the LORD God made to grow every tree that is pleasant to the sight and good for food, the tree of life also in the midst of the garden, and the tree of the knowledge of good and evil.

[10]A river flows out of Eden to water the garden, and from there it divides and becomes four branches. [11]The name of the first is Pishon; it is the one that flows around the whole land of Havilah, where there is gold; [12]and the gold of that land is good; bdellium and onyx stone are there. [13]The name of the second river is Gihon; it is the one that flows around the whole land of Cush. [14]The name of the third river is Tigris, which flows east of Assyria. And the fourth river is the Euphrates.

[15]The LORD God took the man and put him in the garden of Eden to till it and keep it. [16]And the LORD God commanded the man, "You may freely eat of every tree of the garden; [17]but of the tree of the knowledge of good and evil you shall not eat, for in the day that you eat of it you shall die."

Reflection

The Bible teaches that we are of one substance with the soil. We are made from the dust of earth and the breath of God. This teaching echoes in our souls. The wisdom it provides is not disproven by evolutionary theory. As farmer-scientist John Jeavons has said, "Man, despite his artistic pretensions, his sophistication and many accomplishments, owes the fact of his existence to a six-inch layer of topsoil and the fact that it rains." All human life depends on food—and food depends on soil, water and sun: the providence of God's creation. No human being made it; all receive it as gift.

Rich and poor both receive life from God. But rich and poor do not have equal access to nutritious food directly from well-tended soils. Where I live, poor people have easy access to free processed food donated by large companies seeking to manage waste. Strange as it is to say, our widespread obesity epidemic can be traced to past policy decisions that prioritized economic expansion over soil stewardship. Nutritious fresh fruits and vegetables grown in a manner that stewards the soil are harder to find. But wealth shouldn't determine health.

How can we develop an agriculture that treats the soil as gift from God? How can we create a food system that more fully reflects God's grace and abundance, providing not only rain and sun but also fruits and vegetables to the wealthy and the poor alike? In every geographic location, Christians are hard at work seeking answers to these questions. We are rethinking how we source the food we provide to those in need through our charities. We are starting food gardens on church property and creating farm-based ministries. We are asking how we are called to steward the land in our care.

Like us, the soil was created by God for good. As we tend it, we learn our place in God's creation.

The Rev. Nurya Love Parish
Plainsong Farm and Ministry
Grand Rapids, Michigan

Questions_____

What do you know about the natural systems on which your life depends? What would you like to know?

What one small thing can you do to develop a food system that reflects the experience of Holy Communion: where all are fed in a manner which restores relationship between God and our neighbors?

Prayer _____

Holy and Eternal God, you have formed us from the dust of the earth and given us the breath of life. Give us also your wisdom, that we might know our place in your creation. Day by day enable us each to take one next, imperfect, possible step to serve you, even against adversity. This we pray in the name of Christ our Lord, through whom we have been reconciled to you and in whom we find our greatest joy. *Amen*.

Exodus 2:23-25, 3:1-17

²³After a long time the king of Egypt died. The Israelites groaned under their slavery, and cried out. Out of the slavery their cry for help rose up to God. ²⁴God heard their groaning, and God remembered his covenant with Abraham, Isaac, and Jacob. ²⁵God looked upon the Israelites, and God took notice of them.

3 Moses was keeping the flock of his father-in-law Jethro, the priest of Midian; he led his flock beyond the wilderness, and came to Horeb, the mountain of God. ²There the angel of the Lord appeared to him in a flame of fire out of a bush; he looked, and the bush was blazing, yet it was not consumed. ³Then Moses said, "I must turn aside and look at this great sight, and see why the bush is not burned up." ⁴When the Lord saw that he had turned aside to see, God called to him out of the bush, "Moses,

Moses!" And he said, "Here I am." ⁵Then he said, "Come no closer! Remove the sandals from your feet, for the place on which you are standing is holy ground." ⁶He said further, "I am the God of your father, the God of Abraham, the God of Isaac, and the God of Jacob." And Moses hid his face, for he was afraid to look at God.

⁷Then the Lord said, "I have observed the misery of my people who are in Egypt; I have heard their cry on account of their taskmasters. Indeed, I know their sufferings, ⁸and I have come down to deliver them from the Egyptians, and to bring them up out of that land to a good and broad land, a land flowing with milk and honey, to the country of the Canaanites, the Hittites, the Amorites, the Perizzites, the Hivites, and the Jebusites. ⁹The cry of the Israelites has now

come to me; I have also seen how the Egyptians oppress them. [10]So come, I will send you to Pharaoh to bring my people, the Israelites, out of Egypt." [11]But Moses said to God, "Who am I that I should go to Pharaoh, and bring the Israelites out of Egypt?" [12]He said, "I will be with you; and this shall be the sign for you that it is I who sent you: when you have brought the people out of Egypt, you shall worship God on this mountain."

[13]But Moses said to God, "If I come to the Israelites and say to them, 'The God of your ancestors has sent me to you,' and they ask me, 'What is his name?' what shall I say to them?" [14]God said to Moses, "I AM WHO I AM." He said further, "Thus you shall say to the Israelites, 'I AM has sent me to you.'" [15]God also said to Moses, "Thus you shall say to the Israelites, 'The Lord, the God of your ancestors, the God of Abraham, the God of Isaac, and the God of Jacob, has sent me to you': This is my name forever, and this my title for all generations.

[16]Go and assemble the elders of Israel, and say to them, 'The Lord, the God of your ancestors, the God of Abraham, of Isaac, and of Jacob, has appeared to me, saying: I have given heed to you and to what has been done to you in Egypt. [17]I declare that I will bring you up out of the misery of Egypt, to the land of the Canaanites, the Hittites, the Amorites, the Perizzites, the Hivites, and the Jebusites, a land flowing with milk and honey.'"

Reflection

#MyPeople

As I write this meditation in September 2016, Terence Crutcher—black, unarmed, hands up—has just been killed by a police officer. #TerenceCrutcher is all over social media.

Another day, another lynching, another hashtag.

#MikeBrown

#SandraBland

#TerenceCrutcher

Who is it today?

The people of Israel were slaves. Pharaoh saw them not as images of God but as means of production—brown bodies whose labor generated wealth for him. They "groaned under their slavery and cried out" (Exodus 2:23). But nobody heard and nobody did a thing to stop it.

Nobody except God.

God heard. And God looked upon them. And noticed them. And trusted their cries were true.

And God came to Moses and said:

"I have observed the misery of my people who are in Egypt; I have heard their cry on account of their taskmasters. Indeed, I know their sufferings, and I have come down to deliver them."

I am a 47-year-old white man, husband, father and priest. And until Michael Brown was murdered and his body lay in the street in Ferguson, Missouri—for four and a half hours—until mourners were met with police dogs, tear gas and rubber bullets, until young people took to the streets demanding justice and telling their stories of suffering, I always thought this story was about somebody else.

If I had to place myself in this story, I would have said I was Moses... or maybe Aaron.

But now I know. I am Pharaoh.

I participate in, benefit from, and actively sustain—through sins of omission and commission—political, economic, and social systems of white supremacy and patriarchy that keep God's people in bondage, use their labor to generate wealth for the already wealthy, and beat and kill them with impunity.

My ears have been deaf. And my heart has been hard.

I am Pharaoh. And Moses is telling me: "God says, 'Let my people go.'"

The Rev. Mike Kinman
All Saints' Episcopal Church
Pasadena, California

Questions_____

If you are a part of the America of Color, what is your reaction to the story of the conversation between God and Moses in Exodus? What is your cry? How easy is it for you to believe that God hears it?

If you are part of White America, what is your reaction to being cast as Pharaoh in this story? What is it like to consider that Moses is a young, black, queer, profane woman standing in the street with her fist in the air?

God has already written the end of the story—and God's endings are all about liberation. What do you need to do to follow God's call and be a part of God's revolution of liberation? What does your faith community need to do? What action can you commit to right now?

Prayer _____

God, who hears the cries of the people on account of their taskmasters, hear your people now as they cry: No Justice. No Peace. Hands Up. Don't Shoot. If We Don't Get It...Shut It Down! Let My People Go! Comfort and deliver those of us who cry out. Convict and convert those of us who sit on Pharaoh's throne and consecrate all of us to your dream of freedom for all your children. *Amen.*

Exodus 5:1—6:13

5 Afterward Moses and Aaron went to Pharaoh and said, "Thus says the LORD, the God of Israel, 'Let my people go, so that they may celebrate a festival to me in the wilderness.'" ²But Pharaoh said, "Who is the LORD, that I should heed him and let Israel go? I do not know the LORD, and I will not let Israel go." ³Then they said, "The God of the Hebrews has revealed himself to us; let us go a three days' journey into the wilderness to sacrifice to the LORD our God, or he will fall upon us with pestilence or sword."

⁴But the king of Egypt said to them, "Moses and Aaron, why are you taking the people away from their work? Get to your labors!" ⁵Pharaoh continued, "Now they are more numerous than the people of the land and yet you want them to stop working!" ⁶That same day Pharaoh commanded the taskmasters of the people, as well as their supervisors, ⁷"You shall no longer give the people straw to make bricks, as before; let them go and gather straw for themselves. ⁸But you shall require of them the same quantity of bricks as they have made previously; do not diminish it, for they are lazy; that is why they cry, 'Let us go and offer sacrifice to our God.' ⁹Let heavier work be laid on them; then they will labor at it and pay no attention to deceptive words."

¹⁰So the taskmasters and the supervisors of the people went out and said to the people, "Thus says Pharaoh, 'I will not give you straw. ¹¹Go and get straw yourselves, wherever you can find it; but your work will not be lessened in the least.'" ¹²So the people scattered throughout the land of Egypt, to gather stubble

for straw. ¹³The taskmasters were urgent, saying, "Complete your work, the same daily assignment as when you were given straw." ¹⁴And the supervisors of the Israelites, whom Pharaoh's taskmasters had set over them, were beaten, and were asked, "Why did you not finish the required quantity of bricks yesterday and today, as you did before?"

¹⁵Then the Israelite supervisors came to Pharaoh and cried, "Why do you treat your servants like this? ¹⁶No straw is given to your servants, yet they say to us, 'Make bricks!' Look how your servants are beaten! You are unjust to your own people." ¹⁷He said, "You are lazy, lazy; that is why you say, 'Let us go and sacrifice to the Lord.' ¹⁸Go now, and work; for no straw shall be given you, but you shall still deliver the same number of bricks." ¹⁹The Israelite supervisors saw that they were in trouble when they were told, "You shall not lessen your daily number of bricks." ²⁰As they left Pharaoh, they came upon Moses and Aaron who were waiting to meet them. ²¹They said to them, "The LORD look upon you and judge! You have brought us into bad odor with Pharaoh and his officials, and have put a sword in their hand to kill us."

²²Then Moses turned again to the Lord and said, "O LORD, why have you mistreated this people? Why did you ever send me? ²³Since I first came to Pharaoh to speak in your name, he has mistreated this people, and you have done nothing at all to deliver your people."

6 Then the LORD said to Moses, "Now you shall see what I will do to Pharaoh: Indeed, by a mighty hand he will let them go; by a mighty hand he will drive them out of his land."

²God also spoke to Moses and said to him: "I am the LORD. ³I appeared to Abraham, Isaac, and Jacob as God Almighty, but by my name 'The LORD' I did not make myself known to them. ⁴I also established my covenant

with them, to give them the land of Canaan, the land in which they resided as aliens. ⁵I have also heard the groaning of the Israelites whom the Egyptians are holding as slaves, and I have remembered my covenant. ⁶Say therefore to the Israelites, 'I am the LORD, and I will free you from the burdens of the Egyptians and deliver you from slavery to them. I will redeem you with an outstretched arm and with mighty acts of judgment. ⁷I will take you as my people, and I will be your God. You shall know that I am the LORD your God, who has freed you from the burdens of the Egyptians. ⁸I will bring you into the land that I swore to give to Abraham, Isaac, and Jacob; I will give it to you for a possession. I am the Lord.'" ⁹Moses told this to the Israelites; but they would not listen to Moses, because of their broken spirit and their cruel slavery.

¹⁰Then the LORD spoke to Moses, ¹¹"Go and tell Pharaoh king of Egypt to let the Israelites go out of his land." ¹²But Moses spoke to the LORD, "The Israelites have not listened to me; how then shall Pharaoh listen to me, poor speaker that I am?" ¹³Thus the LORD spoke to Moses and Aaron, and gave them orders regarding the Israelites and Pharaoh king of Egypt, charging them to free the Israelites from the land of Egypt.

Reflection

Migration, exodus, and return are important biblical and historical narratives that pose challenging questions about our responsibilities toward and treatment of the other. With more than 65 million people displaced by violence and persecution globally, this passage exemplifies the true nature of our generation's human rights challenge.

There are more people displaced by violence in the world today than at any time since World War II. For many, this crisis is characterized by conflicts in Syria, Iraq, and Afghanistan, and yet the most violent region in the world is much closer than we might think. The Northern Triangle of Central America—El Salvador, Guatemala, and Honduras—recorded 17,500 violent deaths in 2015, and nearly a million individuals were displaced by violence in the Northern Triangle and Mexico.

In El Salvador, I have witnessed first-hand this exodus and return through my work with the historically displaced—the poor. Excluded from the equal exercise of rights, these people suffer directly the consequences of civil war, natural disasters, and the social conflict raging in El Salvador. As this scripture passage shows, the act of displacement—the choice to leave one's home, one's family, to uproot—is not only the result of the threat of direct violence but also of a history of structural violence and exclusion. Sadly, Central Americans who flee violence and persecution today often find themselves caught in cycles of abuse, detention, and deportation rather than finding the protection they sought when they fled their homes.

In this passage, the Lord not only releases the Israelites from Pharaoh's oppression but promises to redeem them through acts of judgment. And yet, because of "discouragement and harsh labor," the Israelites cannot hear Moses' promise. Many families in Central America are unable to access the justice system and are forced to defend their lives in the face of diminishing freedoms. This is the true nature of our challenge today: to not only promise welcome to those who flee violence but also to redeem them, to empower them to exercise their rights to protection and a future full of promise.

Noah F. Bullock
Cristosal
El Salvador

Questions

What injustices do you observe in your local community? Can you identify specific structures (policies, prejudices, lack of services, etc.) that reinforce that injustice?

Put yourself in Moses' shoes at the end of this passage. What might you say to Pharaoh to persuade him?

have compassion

Prayer

God, we gather in prayerful solidarity with the voiceless and vulnerable. May we speak out and take action. We pray for all who strive with optimism in the face of great injustice and crippling poverty and for those who have abandoned hope. We pray for all who have been forced to flee from violence and injustice, for all who are in danger at sea or on land, and for those who cannot escape the chains of poverty, unemployment and intimidation. May we stand in solidarity with all who cry out for mercy, justice and freedom. *Amen.*

Exodus 16:1-36

16 The whole congregation of the Israelites set out from Elim; and Israel came to the wilderness of Sin, which is between Elim and Sinai, on the fifteenth day of the second month after they had departed from the land of Egypt. ²The whole congregation of the Israelites complained against Moses and Aaron in the wilderness. ³The Israelites said to them, "If only we had died by the hand of the LORD in the land of Egypt, when we sat by the fleshpots and ate our fill of bread; for you have brought us out into this wilderness to kill this whole assembly with hunger."

⁴Then the LORD said to Moses, "I am going to rain bread from heaven for you, and each day the people shall go out and gather enough for that day. In that way I will test them, whether they will follow my instruction or not. ⁵On the sixth day, when they prepare what they bring in, it will be twice as much as they gather on other days." ⁶So Moses and Aaron said to all the Israelites, "In the evening you shall know that it was the LORD who brought you out of the land of Egypt, ⁷and in the morning you shall see the glory of the LORD, because he has heard your complaining against the LORD. For what are we, that you complain against us?" ⁸And Moses said, "When the LORD gives you meat to eat in the evening and your fill of bread in the morning, because the Lord has heard the complaining that you utter against him—what are we? Your complaining is not against us but against the LORD."

⁹Then Moses said to Aaron, "Say to the whole congregation of the Israelites, 'Draw near to the LORD, for he has heard your

complaining.'" ¹⁰And as Aaron spoke to the whole congregation of the Israelites, they looked toward the wilderness, and the glory of the LORD appeared in the cloud. ¹¹The LORD spoke to Moses and said, ¹²"I have heard the complaining of the Israelites; say to them, 'At twilight you shall eat meat, and in the morning you shall have your fill of bread; then you shall know that I am the LORD your God.'"

¹³In the evening quails came up and covered the camp; and in the morning there was a layer of dew around the camp. ¹⁴When the layer of dew lifted, there on the surface of the wilderness was a fine flaky substance, as fine as frost on the ground. ¹⁵When the Israelites saw it, they said to one another, "What is it?" For they did not know what it was. Moses said to them, "It is the bread that the LORD has given you to eat. ¹⁶This is what the LORD has commanded: 'Gather as much of it as each of you needs, an omer to a person according to the number of persons, all providing for those in their own tents.'" ¹⁷The Israelites did so, some gathering more, some less. ¹⁸But when they measured it with an omer, those who gathered much had nothing over, and those who gathered little had no shortage; they gathered as much as each of them needed. ¹⁹And Moses said to them, "Let no one leave any of it over until morning." ²⁰But they did not listen to Moses; some left part of it until morning, and it bred worms and became foul. And Moses was angry with them. ²¹Morning by morning they gathered it, as much as each needed; but when the sun grew hot, it melted.

²²On the sixth day they gathered twice as much food, two omers apiece. When all the leaders of the congregation came and told Moses, ²³he said to them, "This is what the LORD has commanded: 'Tomorrow is a day of solemn rest, a holy sabbath to the LORD; bake what you want to bake and boil what you want to boil, and

all that is left over put aside to be kept until morning.'" ²⁴So they put it aside until morning, as Moses commanded them; and it did not become foul, and there were no worms in it. ²⁵Moses said, "Eat it today, for today is a sabbath to the LORD; today you will not find it in the field. ²⁶Six days you shall gather it; but on the seventh day, which is a sabbath, there will be none."

²⁷On the seventh day some of the people went out to gather, and they found none. ²⁸The LORD said to Moses, "How long will you refuse to keep my commandments and instructions? ²⁹See! The LORD has given you the sabbath, therefore on the sixth day he gives you food for two days; each of you stay where you are; do not leave your place on the seventh day." ³⁰So the people rested on the seventh day.

³¹The house of Israel called it manna; it was like coriander seed, white, and the taste of it was like wafers made with honey. ³²Moses said, "This is what the LORD has commanded: 'Let an omer of it be kept throughout your generations, in order that they may see the food with which I fed you in the wilderness, when I brought you out of the land of Egypt.'" ³³And Moses said to Aaron, "Take a jar, and put an omer of manna in it, and place it before the LORD, to be kept throughout your generations." ³⁴As the LORD commanded Moses, so Aaron placed it before the covenant, for safekeeping. ³⁵The Israelites ate manna forty years, until they came to a habitable land; they ate manna, until they came to the border of the land of Canaan. ³⁶An omer is a tenth of an ephah.

Reflection

The narrative of Exodus in chapter 16 takes the reader by surprise. The Israelites have just miraculously escaped from Egypt and witnessed the destruction of Pharaoh's soldiers in the Red Sea. What a triumph! What a song of victory is sung by Moses and the whole congregation—the first congregational song recorded in the Bible. So what goes wrong? Why the complaining, after they have put their trust in the Lord and in Moses his servant (14:31)?

Well, the simple answer is that they are hungry. Their empty bellies cause them to distrust God's care for them. They think back to Egypt and are tempted to consider that the food from the hands of their Egyptian masters is better than the gift of freedom from the hand of the Lord.

Yet God graciously listens to their complaint, unworthy as it is, and rains down food in abundance—quail in the evening and manna in the morning. What a blessing to receive, not as a reward for faithfulness but as a gift of sovereign grace to the undeserving. Reflecting later upon this episode, Moses declares that God has humbled them with hunger, then provided manna in the wilderness so that they might learn that no one lives by bread alone but by every word that proceeds from the mouth of the Lord (Deuteronomy 8:3). In other words, their hunger is a test. In fact, God continues to test the Israelites to trust his words, as the manna for each day only lasts a day, except for the sixth day, when an extra day's ration survives unblemished for the sabbath day of rest. Some do not pass this test. Yet God continues to provide them manna, their daily bread of heaven, and does so for forty years until the children of Israel arrive in the Promised Land.

The Most Rev. Glenn N. Davies
Diocese of Sydney
Anglican Church of Australia

Questions

What is God's purpose in testing the Israelites with hunger?

How have you been tested by God—and have you seen God's provision in unimaginable ways?

Since God is a God who supplies all our needs, how might we imitate God in supplying the needs of others?

Prayer

God, we thank you for all your gifts so freely bestowed upon us. Strengthen us by your Holy Spirit to live our lives in dependence upon your word, and enable us to share with others of the bounty of your grace, in word and deed, to the glory of the Lord Jesus. *Amen.*

Exodus 23:1-13

23 You shall not spread a false report. You shall not join hands with the wicked to act as a malicious witness. ²You shall not follow a majority in wrongdoing; when you bear witness in a lawsuit, you shall not side with the majority so as to pervert justice; ³nor shall you be partial to the poor in a lawsuit.

⁴When you come upon your enemy's ox or donkey going astray, you shall bring it back.

⁵When you see the donkey of one who hates you lying under its burden and you would hold back from setting it free, you must help to set it free. ⁶You shall not pervert the justice due to your poor in their lawsuits. ⁷Keep far from a false charge, and do not kill the innocent and those in the right, for I will not acquit the guilty. ⁸You shall take no bribe, for a bribe blinds the officials, and subverts the cause of those who are in the right. ⁹You shall not oppress a resident alien; you know the heart of an alien, for you were aliens in the land of Egypt.

¹⁰For six years you shall sow your land and gather in its yield; ¹¹but the seventh year you shall let it rest and lie fallow, so that the poor of your people may eat; and what they leave the wild animals may eat. You shall do the same with your vineyard, and with your olive orchard.

¹²Six days you shall do your work, but on the seventh day you shall rest, so that your ox and your donkey may have relief, and your homeborn slave and the resident alien may be refreshed. ¹³Be attentive to all that I have said to you. Do not invoke the names of other gods; do not let them be heard on your lips.

Reflection

Let there be equal justice.

The scripture in these passages outlines the way of being a community that God has laid out for the children of Israel. The "you shall nots" further define the direction in which God expects the people to offer their lives to the world.

The prophet Amos will later bring God's message of justice to the people: "I hate, I despise your festivals, and I take no delight in your solemn assemblies. Take away from me the noise of your songs; I will not listen to the melody of your harps. But let justice roll down like waters, and righteousness like an everflowing stream" (Amos 5:21, 23-24). There is no doubt about what God is looking for from the people, just as we have no doubts about being called to love God and our neighbors.

The Baptismal Covenant directs us "to seek and serve Christ in all persons…to strive for justice and peace among all people…" Yet, it is difficult to see justice today on an equal level for all God's people. Justice seems to be meted out according to the color of one's skin— young children who are underserved in ill-equipped classrooms and young people profiled because they look suspicious.

In my ministry with young people, I listen to their fears, sharing their tears and frustrations as they struggle to come to grips with how they are perceived by others, notwithstanding their own perspectives of themselves. They experience double-standard responses: a parent is called into a situation on the one hand, and on the other, classmates are handcuffed and arrested without a parent in sight, all based on skin color.

The church has much wisdom to offer in dealing with each other. We have no shortage of teachings and avenues for our legislative bodies to call for drastic changes in a system that is broken. Will the church become the village that raises up children and becomes the gang of choice for our young people? God has given us all we need and reminds us that with God's grace, we can do infinitely more than we can ask or imagine.

The Rev. Canon Angela S. Ifill
Office of Black Ministries
The Episcopal Church

Questions

In what ways can you personally address injustices in your local community?

How can your community of faith address local injustices?

What can you do to provide a safe and loving place for young people?

Prayer

O God, you know our hearts and you know our needs before we ask. Engender in us hearts for your people and the courage to move beyond that which is comfortable, knowing that you have already prepared us for the work you have given us to do. Remind us of those who are less fortunate, the powerless, the needy, and especially the little ones among us. Give us grace, dear Lord, to do your will, and to your glory may we become exemplars of your love and care for all people. These things we ask in your name. *Amen.*

Leviticus 19:1-18, 32-37; 23:22

19 The LORD spoke to Moses, saying: ²Speak to all the congregation of the people of Israel and say to them: You shall be holy, for I the LORD your God am holy. ³You shall each revere your mother and father, and you shall keep my sabbaths: I am the LORD your God. ⁴Do not turn to idols or make cast images for yourselves: I am the LORD your God.

⁵When you offer a sacrifice of well-being to the LORD, offer it in such a way that it is acceptable on your behalf. ⁶It shall be eaten on the same day you offer it, or on the next day; and anything left over until the third day shall be consumed in fire. ⁷If it is eaten at all on the third day, it is an abomination; it will not be acceptable. ⁸All who eat it shall be subject to punishment, because they have profaned what is holy to the LORD; and any

such person shall be cut off from the people. ⁹When you reap the harvest of your land, you shall not reap to the very edges of your field, or gather the gleanings of your harvest. ¹⁰You shall not strip your vineyard bare, or gather the fallen grapes of your vineyard; you shall leave them for the poor and the alien: I am the LORD your God.

¹¹You shall not steal; you shall not deal falsely; and you shall not lie to one another. ¹²And you shall not swear falsely by my name, profaning the name of your God: I am the LORD.

¹³You shall not defraud your neighbor; you shall not steal; and you shall not keep for yourself the wages of a laborer until morning. ¹⁴You shall not revile the deaf or put a stumbling block before the blind; you shall fear your God: I am the LORD.

¹⁵You shall not render an unjust judgment; you shall not be partial to the poor or defer to the great: with justice you shall judge your neighbor. ¹⁶You shall not go around as a slanderer among your people, and you shall not profit by the blood of your neighbor: I am the LORD.

¹⁷You shall not hate in your heart anyone of your kin; you shall reprove your neighbor, or you will incur guilt yourself. ¹⁸You shall not take vengeance or bear a grudge against any of your people, but you shall love your neighbor as yourself: I am the LORD...

³²You shall rise before the aged, and defer to the old; and you shall fear your God: I am the LORD. ³³When an alien resides with you in your land, you shall not oppress the alien. ³⁴The alien who resides with you shall be to you as the citizen among you; you shall love the alien as yourself, for you were aliens in the land of Egypt: I am the LORD your God.

³⁵You shall not cheat in measuring length, weight, or quantity. ³⁶You shall have honest balances, honest weights, an honest ephah, and an honest hin: I am the LORD your God, who brought you out of the land of Egypt. ³⁷You shall keep all my statutes and all my ordinances, and observe them: I am the LORD...

²²When you reap the harvest of your land, you shall not reap to the very edges of your field, or gather the gleanings of your harvest; you shall leave them for the poor and for the alien: I am the LORD your God.

Reflection

The legal material in the book of Leviticus is punctuated with the phrases "I am the LORD your God" and "I the LORD your God am holy." If we learn nothing else about God in Leviticus, it is clear that the people belong to a holy God and God's holiness makes demands on them. Throughout the book of Leviticus, God calls the people to holiness again and again.

What does holiness look like? We Christians have struggled and debated this question for centuries, attempting to sort through the layers of cultural norms, societal mores, and God's intentions for us. Today, I am interested in those parts of the holiness code that don't need explanation. In Leviticus, one clear way to demonstrate that we are the people of God, emulating holiness, is by allowing the practice of gleaning. Scripture instructs farmers and vintners not to harvest all of their produce. They are to refrain from reaping or harvesting to the "very edges of your field." And they are forbidden to strip their "vineyards bare, or gather the fallen grapes." Rather they are to intentionally leave some of the harvest for the "poor and the alien."

Scripture is clear on this matter, repeating these instructions in Leviticus. The underpinnings of this commandment are based in two assumptions: What we have comes from God, and it is not God's intention for us to merely accumulate material goods for ourselves. Part of belonging to God means sharing that with which we have been blessed.

Many of our churches offer assistance to those in need, in our communities and beyond. Many of us tithe or pledge from our income to help offset the cost of this work. The commandment in Leviticus, however, is geared toward a worldview that runs counter-cultural to American consumerism and many of our policies about benevolence. Gleaning isn't a handout and never was—it's an invitation to the poor and the immigrant to participate in and benefit from the harvest. So many of us are comfortable giving something to someone in need and sending them away, but gleaning is an action that invites the outsider to become a part of the community and receive God's blessings.

Gleaning reminds us that we are recipients of God's blessings—none of it is ours and it all comes from God. We don't give because it is ours to give. We give because it is not ours; we too have gleaned in God's fields and vineyards. Gleaning reminds us that we were strangers to God, that we became a part of God's family through God's grace, and that there is plenty to share.

The Rev. Judy Fentress-Williams
Virginia Theological Seminary
Alexandria, Virginia

Questions

How do our benevolence programs invite people in? What would the world economy look like if we followed the Levitical commands about land usage and harvesting practices?

What blessings come to us when we are obedient to God by sharing our blessings?

Prayer

Lord, help us always to remember the doxology, "Praise God from whom all blessings flow..." Keep always in our minds our own stories of wandering and adoption, so that as we give, we celebrate the story of your mercy toward all your people. *Amen.*

2 Kings 4:1-7

4 Now the wife of a member of the company of prophets cried to Elisha, "Your servant my husband is dead; and you know that your servant feared the LORD, but a creditor has come to take my two children as slaves." ²Elisha said to her, "What shall I do for you? Tell me, what do you have in the house?" She answered, "Your servant has nothing in the house, except a jar of oil." ³He said, "Go outside, borrow vessels from all your neighbors, empty vessels and not just a few. ⁴Then go in, and shut the door behind you and your children, and start pouring into all these vessels; when each is full, set it aside." ⁵So she left him and shut the door behind her and her children; they kept bringing vessels to her, and she kept pouring. ⁶When the vessels were full, she said to her son, "Bring me another vessel." But he said to her, "There are no more." Then the oil stopped flowing. ⁷She came and told the man of God, and he said, "Go sell the oil and pay your debts, and you and your children can live on the rest."

Reflection

Around the world today, more than 3 billion people live in poverty and 1.3 billion struggle to survive on less than $1.25 a day. The vulnerable poor are especially subject to disease, death, and oppression. The Bible expresses God's concern for the defense and care of widows, orphans, and refugees. Elisha's encounter with the widow provides a biblical model for transformational ministry among the poor.

In the midst of his ministry to the kings of Israel, Elisha empowers an impoverished widow. The miracle of oil begins with a widow's plea and results in divine deliverance and an escape from poverty. The prophet's questions to the widow are striking: "What shall I do for you?" and "What do you have in the house?"

Christian ministry is about helping others, but that help must be understood contextually and give voice to the marginalized and weak in their own homes. "Your servant has nothing in the house, except a jar of oil," the widow replies.

Poverty often fails to recognize available resources. Who knew that a few drops of oil could feed a family for months? The widow's active faith is expressed through her collection and filling of empty jars. The community is engaged and contributes to the welfare of a neighbor in need. Through the widow's work, a business is born and a family saved. God's all-sufficient grace is poured into neglect and need, and abundance is the result.

My organization has worked with twenty countries, focusing on areas of extreme poverty in some of the most overlooked parts of the world. In every community, no matter how desperate the situation, we have always found a host of local resources available and ready to be developed. As members come together in faith and learn to recognize, develop, and mobilize local talents and resources, they find that the solution to poverty begins in their own homes. Resources committed and mobilized to the work of God find blessing and multiplication.

Sonia H. Patterson
Five Talents, USA
Washington, D.C.

Questions _____

Who are the vulnerable poor in your community?

How can the church engage and empower the poor in sustainable transformations?

Prayer _____

God, we pray that you will be with us. Sustain us in what we do for those to whom you lead us. Expand our territory and influence for your glory, in Jesus' Name. *Amen.*

Psalm 41:1-13

¹Happy are they who consider the poor and needy! *
  the LORD will deliver them in the time of trouble.

²The LORD preserves them and keeps them alive,
so that they may be happy in the land; *
  he does not hand them over to the will of their enemies.

³The LORD sustains them on their sickbed *
  and ministers to them in their illness.

⁴I said, "LORD, be merciful to me; heal me, *
  for I have sinned against you."

⁵My enemies are saying wicked things about me: *
  "When will he die, and his name perish?"

⁶Even if they come to see me, they speak empty words; *
  their heart collects false rumors; they go outside
    and spread them.

⁷All my enemies whisper together about me *
  and devise evil against me.

⁸"A deadly thing," they say, has fastened on him; *
  he has taken to his bed and will never get up again."

⁹Even my best friend, whom I trusted,
who broke bread with me, *
  has lifted up his heel and turned against me.

¹⁰But you, O LORD, be merciful to me and raise me up, *
  and I shall repay them.

[11]By this I know you are pleased with me, *

    that my enemy does not triumph over me.

[12]In my integrity you hold me fast, *

    and shall set me before your face for ever.

[13]Blessed be the LORD God of Israel, *

    from age to age. Amen. Amen.

Reflection

As we see in Psalm 41, concern for the poor, weak, and marginalized is at the heart of a life shaped by justice, prayer, and faith. The piety and action of a follower of God are animated by these concerns.

It is in and among the poor that we are to practice our faith. God places our deepest spiritual needs in the life of the poor and marginalized. We meet the Messiah in the poor and marginalized (Matthew 25:31-). We must serve the marginalized, as we seek our Savior.

Our challenge is to make our concern for the poor an integral part of what it means to be individual disciples of Christ and part of communities of faith. The suburbanization of churches makes this difficult. Very few of the poor can afford to attend our churches. Our churches are not sustainable in their present situations among the poor. Further, much of our outreach to the poor and marginalized does not involve real engagement or community. Because the outreach is at arm's length, the mutuality of real community is missing. This must change if we are to rediscover the blessedness found among the poor.

The Rt. Rev. Mark MacDonald
National Indigenous Anglican Bishop in Canada

Questions

Could a marginalized person become active in your congregation? How easy would this be? What steps could you take to make it easier?

How could a church become viable within a poor or marginalized community?

Prayer

Almighty God, in your Son's embrace of poverty, you gave us the riches of a divine life. As you have promised, meet us in the poor and marginalized and help us to meet you in them, through the same Jesus Christ our Lord. *Amen.*

Psalm 72:12-14

[12]For he shall deliver the poor who cries out in distress, *
    and the oppressed who has no helper.

[13]He shall have pity on the lowly and poor; *
    he shall preserve the lives of the needy.

[14]He shall redeem their lives from oppression and violence, *
    and dear shall their blood be in his sight.

Reflection

Every society has a shadow side, and sometimes the darkness is caused by a superstition. While serving as a volunteer Episcopal missionary teaching in Eldorett, Kenya, I learned of a belief that causes much pain and suffering. Often children born in rural Kenya with a physical disability are considered a curse, and the mothers are blamed.

The birth of a child with a club foot, cerebral palsy, or similar disability casts shame on the families. Sometimes the shame is so great that the father deserts the family, leaving the mother and child destitute. These children are hidden and rarely taken out in public. Imagine the isolated life of such a child, the sadness and desperation of the mother. These children who are hidden from sight are the poorest and neediest of any people I have met in my work because they live without hope.

How does God care for these children and mothers? One way God's mercy and care came to Kenya was in 1990 when a woman named Percia Hutcherson was invited by an Anglican bishop to come to the Diocese of Eldoret. Percia, a retired physical therapist, founded the North Rift Rehabilitation Center to provide treatment for children with disabilities. Percia's legacy continues today.

God delivered the poor and needy of Eldoret by calling Percia and inspiring her to share her professional expertise and teach Kenyans how to carry forward this compassionate work. Many lives have been made healthy and hopeful because they received care through the rehabilitation center.

I have witnessed how a few dedicated people make miraculous differences in the lives of the neediest children and mothers. The lessons for me are about the miracles that can be accomplished when we share our gifts and knowledge with each other. By doing so, we become agents of God's care for those in need.

Mary M. and Jim Higbee
Episcopal Missionaries
South Sudan

Questions

Who comes to mind when you think of the poor and needy?

What skills and abilities do you have that would make a difference in the lives of those you named?

In what ways can you pray for those in need? How will you discern a call to offer care?

Prayer

Gracious Lord, thank you for giving me spiritual gifts, abilities, and skills. Inspire in me the courage and strength to step forward and offer what I can. Let me see the poor and needy through the lens of your compassion and mercy. *Amen.*

Psalm 102:1-17

¹LORD, hear my prayer, and let my cry come before you; *
  hide not your face from me in the day of my trouble.

²Incline your ear to me; *
  when I call, make haste to answer me,

³For my days drift away like smoke, *
  and my bones are hot as burning coals.

⁴My heart is smitten like grass and withered, *
  so that I forget to eat my bread.

⁵Because of the voice of my groaning *
  I am but skin and bones.

⁶I have become like a vulture in the wilderness, *
  like an owl among the ruins.

⁷I lie awake and groan; *
  I am like a sparrow, lonely on a house-top.

⁸My enemies revile me all day long, *
  and those who scoff at me have taken an oath against me.

⁹For I have eaten ashes for bread *
  and mingled my drink with weeping.

¹⁰Because of your indignation and wrath *
  you have lifted me up and thrown me away.

¹¹My days pass away like a shadow, *
  and I wither like the grass.

¹²But you, O Lord, endure for ever, *
    and your Name from age to age.

¹³You will arise and have compassion on Zion,
for it is time to have mercy upon her; *
    indeed, the appointed time has come.

¹⁴For your servants love her very rubble, *
    and are moved to pity even for her dust.

¹⁵The nations shall fear your Name, O Lord, *
    and all the kings of the earth your glory.

¹⁶For the Lord will build up Zion, *
    and his glory will appear.

¹⁷ He will look with favor on the prayer of the homeless; *
    he will not despise their plea.

Reflection

Frank staggers toward the circle, his face bruised and swollen from being attacked earlier in the week. Deborah sits with her head down, her skeletal body scarred with needle marks. Lisa and Jamar push baby Ronnie in a rundown stroller. Some fifty to seventy-five of God's people, most of whom live in tents or on the street, gather weekly for Holy Eucharist on a vacant city lot, the noise of traffic competing with voices at prayer.

Prayers are offered for friends who have died in the past week, mothers who are ill, children who are hungry. Bill's prayer is always the same, "That I wake up tomorrow." Hands reach out expectantly for Christ's

Body and Blood, hands bearing the filth of life on the streets, the callouses and burns of hard living. The deacon dismisses us, "Go in peace to love and serve the Lord!" and the people shout with joy, "THANKS BE TO GOD."

How can people so beaten down by life cry out with joy to the Lord? The superscription to Psalm 102 reads, "A prayer of one afflicted, when faint and pleading before the Lord." A psalm any member of Street Church could have written, the prayer begins as a personal lament, a cry for God's mercy. The psalmist suffers hunger, isolation, humiliation, and grief, at one moment deriding God as the cause of suffering, then interrupting the lament with praise and thanksgiving for the enduring presence of God. The psalmist shifts between an individual lament to a complaint on behalf of all of Zion and back to individual prayer. The needs of one cannot be separated from the needs of the whole. God's mercy will not be denied.

Those of us who live with privilege can seldom fathom either the depth of despair or faith expressed by our StreetChurch congregation. Our members will not be defined by rejection, abuse, and alienation but rather by an unshakable trust in God's grace and compassion. Echoing the psalmist, the cries of despair turn to shouts of joy as we remember that God hears our prayers.

The Rev. Lee Anne Reat
St. John's Episcopal Church
Columbus, Ohio

Questions _____

The psalmist weaves together personal and corporate lament. How are the cries for mercy of the afflicted in your community tied to your own cries for justice?

In your own life of prayer, do your laments turn to praise?

How are you "afflicted," "faint and pleading before the Lord?" Can you praise God in the midst of pain?

Prayer _____

Merciful God, your children cry to you night and day. Open our ears to hear their cries, open our eyes to see your love for all your children; open our hearts to the work of transforming unjust systems. Increase in each of us the gifts of faith, hope, and love, through your Son Jesus Christ. *Amen.*

Proverbs 2:6-9

⁶For the LORD gives wisdom;
from his mouth come
knowledge and understanding;

⁷he stores up sound wisdom for
the upright; he is a shield to
those who walk blamelessly,

⁸guarding the paths of justice
and preserving the way of his
faithful ones.

⁹Then you will understand
righteousness and justice and
equity, every good path;

Reflection

As I write this reflection I am in the city of Philadelphia, Pennsylvania, attending a conference with my wife. This morning I had the opportunity to visit Independence Hall as well as exhibits depicting the Underground Railroad.

As I think about today's passage from Proverbs, I am reminded of the song "America the Beautiful" as sung by Ray Charles. His soulful singing always reminds me that everything I hold dear is a gift from God.

Just as the framers of the Constitution sought freedom from the oppressive control of King George III, my life and ministry has evolved around eradicating the oppressive nature of Jim Crowism, racism, and other societal practices in which human beings see some people as "other" and not as children of the same creator.

Just as the framers heard the voice of God and mustered the courage to conceive a more perfect union based on liberty and the pursuit of happiness for all people, that dream will only be realized when each succeeding generation listens to our better selves and knows that God is always guiding us along the path toward justice.

John E. Harris Jr.
Union of Black Episcopalians
Cincinnati, Ohio

Questions

How is the church today helping human beings see each other as brothers and sisters equal in the eyes of God?

How do we remove oppressive policies and practices from our governments and institutions?

Knowing that God is always leading humankind toward the path of justice, how can we embrace each other with kindness and care? What would we look like as a society?

Prayer

God, we seek your guidance to practice our faith this day. Keep us mindful of your covenant and teachings that we are to provide hospitality to the strangers in our midst; that we maintain solidarity with the poor; and that our work is always to remove obstacles and hindrances to those who are marginalized by society. *Amen.*

Isaiah 41:17-20

[17]When the poor and needy seek water, and there is none, and their tongue is parched with thirst, I the LORD will answer them, I the God of Israel will not forsake them. [18]I will open rivers on the bare heights, and fountains in the midst of the valleys; I will make the wilderness a pool of water, and the dry land springs of water. [19]I will put in the wilderness the cedar, the acacia, the myrtle, and the olive; I will set in the desert the cypress, the plane and the pine together, [20]so that all may see and know, all may consider and understand, that the hand of the LORD has done this, the Holy One of Israel has created it.

Reflection

In our work at Episcopal Community Services, we ask individuals (participants, employees, and stakeholders) to "Look Up" and "Challenge Poverty." We base our work on four core values: dignity, justice, impact, and community. Poverty robs individuals of the dignity of choice; our work is about restoring dignity by creating equal access to opportunities and helping individuals realize their potential.

This passage from Isaiah speaks to the poor who are in search of the most basic of needs: water. Finding none, they grow parched. The Lord responds by providing not only access to the miracle of water in the wilderness but also shade and the olive tree, an ancient symbol of peace. The Lord indeed answers them.

As a faith-based social service agency, we are called to do the Lord's work. While we don't dig wells and tend trees, our call is to build shelter; provide education, employment assistance, wellness, and financial security; and advocate on behalf of those who have no voice.

We do not—and cannot—do this work alone. We try to carry out our ministry "so that all may see and know, all may consider and understand, that the hand of the Lord has done this." We are humbled and grateful that at this time and place we are so called by Jesus for this work. In the arid land of poverty, we look to dig wells and help quench our fellow man's thirst with living water.

David E. Griffith
Episcopal Community Services
Philadelphia, Pennsylvania

Questions

How do you quench the thirst of your neighbors in need?

How can justice and equal access to opportunity be opened by your actions?

Prayer

Lord God, maker of all things, we ask you to make straight the way for us to love our neighbors as ourselves, to do your work wherever there is need, to know that we are one with you and each other on this journey, and that through you, no work will be impossible. *Amen*.

Isaiah 42:1-7

42 Here is my servant, whom I uphold, my chosen, in whom my soul delights; I have put my spirit upon him; he will bring forth justice to the nations. ²He will not cry or lift up his voice, or make it heard in the street; ³a bruised reed he will not break, and a dimly burning wick he will not quench; he will faithfully bring forth justice. ⁴He will not grow faint or be crushed until he has established justice in the earth; and the coastlands wait for his teaching.

⁵Thus says God, the LORD, who created the heavens and stretched them out, who spread out the earth and what comes from it, who gives breath to the people upon it and spirit to those who walk in it: ⁶I am the LORD, I have called you in righteousness, I have taken you by the hand and kept you; I have given you as a covenant to the people, a light to the nations, ⁷to open the eyes that are blind, to bring out the prisoners from the dungeon, from the prison those who sit in darkness.

Reflection

The Song of the Servant in Isaiah 42 invites us to a covenant with God and calls us to be a light to the nations, to open the eyes of the blind, and to bring out the prisoners from dungeons and darkness."

But how can we live into this covenant? Few of us can heal the blind and fewer still have ever even been to a prison. How can one individual make a difference?

Years ago, when our ministry was funded by the United States Agency for International Development to fight HIV/AIDS, we were told that we needed agreements from our African host countries to work with their citizens. Officials in Washington said agreements could take years to obtain. Working with Archbishop Ndongo Ndugane, we were able—in three days—to obtain host country concurrence from the governments of South Africa, Mozambique, and Namibia. On the third day, in the office of the Namibian Minister of Health, I shared our government's warning that agreement could take years. "Yes," he replied, "but the difference is that you are Anglicans—people of faith. During the time of troubles, you stood and told the truth, without regard for your personal well-being, and we trust you."

I felt goosebumps rise on my skin. I knew he wasn't speaking of me— we had never met. The trouble he mentioned was apartheid. And those who had stood and told the truth were Archbishop Desmond Tutu and a host of others. We were simply standing in—and now sharing—the light they had brought to the nations.

This is God's light. When we share it with others, God opens eyes and frees them from the prison of spiritual emptiness. We don't have to be Nobel Peace Prize winners like Desmond Tutu. We simply need to add what we can to the light-giving witness of the body of God's faithful.

The Rev. Canon Robert V. Lee III
Fresh Ministries and Be The Change International
Jacksonville, Florida

Questions

What can you do today in your normal comings and goings that might help spread God's light to those around you?

Who in your life has brought God's light to your life? How can you add to that light and share it with others?

Prayer

Creator God, open my heart to your light. Envelop me with your love, empower me with your Holy Spirit, and guide me into your holy covenant as you help me to be the servant you have created me to be. All this I pray in the Name of Jesus. *Amen.*

Isaiah 58:6-14

⁶Is not this the fast that I choose: to loose the bonds of injustice, to undo the thongs of the yoke, to let the oppressed go free, and to break every yoke? ⁷Is it not to share your bread with the hungry, and bring the homeless poor into your house; when you see the naked, to cover them, and not to hide yourself from your own kin? ⁸Then your light shall break forth like the dawn, and your healing shall spring up quickly; your vindicator shall go before you, the glory of the LORD shall be your rear guard. ⁹Then you shall call, and the LORD will answer; you shall cry for help, and he will say, Here I am.

If you remove the yoke from among you, the pointing of the finger, the speaking of evil, ¹⁰if you offer your food to the hungry and satisfy the needs of the afflicted, then your light shall rise in the darkness and your gloom be like the noonday. ¹¹The LORD will guide you continually, and satisfy your needs in parched places, and make your bones strong; and you shall be like a watered garden, like a spring of water, whose waters never fail. ¹²Your ancient ruins shall be rebuilt; you shall raise up the foundations of many generations; you shall be called the repairer of the breach, the restorer of streets to live in.

¹³If you refrain from trampling the sabbath, from pursuing your own interests on my holy day; if you call the sabbath a delight and the holy day of the LORD honorable; if you honor it, not going your own ways, serving your own interests, or pursuing your own affairs; ¹⁴then you shall

take delight in the LORD, and I will make you ride upon the heights of the earth; I will feed you with the heritage of your ancestor Jacob, for the mouth of the LORD has spoken.

Reflection

Food and hunger are the main focus of Isaiah 58. Fasting is a central part of faith during the time of Isaiah—as long as you have enough food. The poor fast whether they like it or not. The fast God calls for is to provide food for the hungry, to help them break their involuntary fast. It is a fast of doing more instead of less: sharing food, breaking chains, freeing the oppressed, canceling debts, clothing the naked, and being present for our families, friends, and neighbors.

God is pretty clear about these expectations to be "repairers of the breach." But our natural inclination to make sure our own hunger is sated while others are starving can make obedience a challenge. It is easy to fast when our fridge is full and we have a regular paycheck. The hard part of fasting is trusting God enough to empty out our own pantries and help meet the needs of others.

This lesson is driven home time and time again as I visit Episcopal Relief & Development's global program partners. One memorable occasion was during a visit to a village in Ghana. The chief, on behalf of the village, told me that they wanted to give me an elephant as a gesture of thanks as that was the grandest gift they could imagine to show how important our partnership was to them. However, they were too poor to give me an elephant. Instead, all of the family heads of the village decided the most valuable thing that they could give me to show their gratitude (and share their fast) was to collect all of the eggs laid that day and present them to me in a bowl.

Those eggs represented the entire village's wealth for that day, and while it wasn't very much, it was everything they had. And they wanted to share it with me. "This is the kind of fast day I'm after" (Isaiah 58:6, *The Message*).

Robert W. Radtke
Episcopal Relief & Development
New York City, New York

Questions _____

Reflect on the moments you have received a bowl of eggs. Maybe a phone call from a friend when you needed it or someone offering their seat on the bus after an exhausting day at work. How did the gift make you feel?

What can you do today to observe a holy fast by being generous with those hungry and homeless in your community?

Prayer _____

God, we pray for the poor, the hungry, and the neglected throughout the world, that their cries for daily bread may inspire works of compassion and mercy among those to whom much has been given. Give us strength to do justice, love mercy, and walk humbly with you as we respond to the call to heal a hurting world. *Amen.*

Isaiah 61:1-11

61 The spirit of the LORD God is upon me, because the LORD has anointed me; he has sent me to bring good news to the oppressed, to bind up the brokenhearted, to proclaim liberty to the captives, and release to the prisoners; ²to proclaim the year of the Lord's favor, and the day of vengeance of our God; to comfort all who mourn; ³to provide for those who mourn in Zion— to give them a garland instead of ashes, the oil of gladness instead of mourning, the mantle of praise instead of a faint spirit. They will be called oaks of righteousness, the planting of the LORD, to display his glory. ⁴They shall build up the ancient ruins, they shall raise up the former devastations; they shall repair the ruined cities, the devastations of many generations.

⁵Strangers shall stand and feed your flocks, foreigners shall till your land and dress your vines; ⁶but you shall be called priests of the LORD, you shall be named ministers of our God; you shall enjoy the wealth of the nations, and in their riches you shall glory. ⁷Because their shame was double, and dishonor was proclaimed as their lot, therefore they shall possess a double portion; everlasting joy shall be theirs.

⁸For I the LORD love justice, I hate robbery and wrongdoing; I will faithfully give them their recompense, and I will make an everlasting covenant with them. ⁹Their descendants shall be known among the nations, and their offspring among the peoples; all who see them shall acknowledge that they are a people whom the LORD has blessed.

[10]I will greatly rejoice in the LORD, my whole being shall exult in my God; for he has clothed me with the garments of salvation, he has covered me with the robe of righteousness, as a bridegroom decks himself with a garland, and as a bride adorns herself with her jewels. [11]For as the earth brings forth its shoots, and as a garden causes what is sown in it to spring up, so the Lord GOD will cause righteousness and praise to spring up before all the nations.

Reflection

When Nasir came into his new apartment, he experienced the good news of release from captivity. His new home was located in the Francis House of Peace, a permanent supportive housing residence for people who had experienced homelessness, named in honor of Pope Francis. The apartment marked an end to years of homelessness and instability and to the social stigma and rejection Nasir faced as a young gay man. "It's fantastic to look around and say, 'This is really mine,' and to know nobody is going to yell at me to get out."

In this passage from Isaiah, the prophet is addressing the Israelites who are returning to their homeland after a bitter generation in exile. They have experienced liberation from captivity but now have to rebuild the ruined cities and devastated buildings.

The prophet speaks of "the acceptable year of the Lord," a reference to the great Jubilee prescribed by God's covenant with the Israelites (Leviticus 25, Deuteronomy 15). This moment of homecoming is in fact an opportunity to build a social order rooted in God's call for justice.

Five hundred years later, Luke uses this prophetic text as Jesus' inaugural address, setting the tone for his ministry. Ironically, Luke addresses his gospel to a community that includes many wealthy and powerful people (beginning with "most excellent Theophilus"). Luke is making the powerful assertion that good news to the poor is good news for all of us.

Ultimately, we are all in need of liberation from social systems that seduce us into accepting false values, fracture human community, and divide us along economic and racial lines. The biblical Jubilee is in a strict sense a redistribution of wealth, which is certainly a challenge for our modern world. But more fundamentally, the Jubilee is—and was—a restoration of community, in which every one of us has what we need in a shared abundance, and therefore every person can more readily affirm each other's dignity as members of a community.

Our efforts to end homelessness and poverty make us all more human and make our society stronger. As we rebuild our ruined cities, we become like strong oaks of righteousness. None of us are home until all of us are home.

When Nasir came home, we found ourselves closer to home. We were all a little closer to the acceptable year of the Lord, to the blessed Jubilee. And that is good news for all of us.

Sister Mary Scullion
Project HOME
Philadelphia, Pennsylvania

Will O'Brien
The Alternative Seminary
Philadelphia, Pennsylvania

Questions

What do you identify as your own captivity? It may be social, personal, or spiritual.

For those who are economically secure, how do our struggles relate to the struggles of our sisters and brothers who experience poverty, homelessness, and social marginalization?

What does good news for the poor and oppressed mean for our society today? In what ways would it be good news for all of us?

Prayer

God of justice, help us understand how we contribute to the captivity of others. Help us recognize the ways we need liberation, and anoint us with your Spirit, as you did Jesus, so we may work joyfully for the liberation of all of your people. *Amen.*

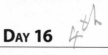

Jeremiah 5:23-30

²³But this people has a stubborn and rebellious heart; they have turned aside and gone away. ²⁴They do not say in their hearts, "Let us fear the Lord our God, who gives the rain in its season, the autumn rain and the spring rain, and keeps for us the weeks appointed for the harvest." ²⁵Your iniquities have turned these away, and your sins have deprived you of good. ²⁶For scoundrels are found among my people; they take over the goods of others. Like fowlers they set a trap; they catch human beings. ²⁷Like a cage full of birds, their houses are full of treachery; therefore they have become great and rich, ²⁸they have grown fat and sleek. They know no limits in deeds of wickedness; they do not judge with justice the cause of the orphan, to make it prosper, and they do not defend the rights of the needy. ²⁹Shall I not punish them for these things? says the Lord, and shall I not bring retribution on a nation such as this? ³⁰An appalling and horrible thing has happened in the land.

Reflection

Reading this passage from Jeremiah reminds me of something that I once read: *A person who lives a moral life is the one who empties himself or herself, denying oneself for the sake of others. It is in emptying ourselves that we find our own life.* When I read this, I reacted by creating a defense mechanism for myself and concluded that since I am not a missionary, I don't need to empty myself. I thought to myself, "It is only Jesus who sacrificed himself for others. I don't have to do this."

Yet Jeremiah says we cannot escape this message. The core indictment of Jeremiah's message painfully accuses those in authority, whether it be in political power, social power, economic power, or in powerful places in the church. This message is about the utter corruption of God's people. There is a tendency for people in powerful positions to no longer fear the Lord because they are filled with pride. They do not fear the Lord who has blessed them. They abuse their authority and accumulate wealth at the expense of the poor. The Bible insists that the ruling class must be examples of a faith that transcends social, political, racial, sexual, and economic divisions.

Jeremiah reminds those in authority that they should neither neglect nor forget those under them who placed them in positions of leadership. Jeremiah reminds us—as well as the powerful—of what happens when calamity and corruption come to leaders. There will be disaster, great trouble, days of misfortune, ruin, torture, and agony if these leaders do not repent and focus on justice for all.

The Rev. Canon Vicentia Kgabe
College of Transfiguration
Grahamstown, South Africa

Questions

In order to truly live morally and justly, it is important for us to empty ourselves for the sake of others. How do you empty yourself so that God may fill you and you may be an instrument in the service of God?

In which ways can we empty and deny ourselves so that we may be of greater help to others in their troubles?

Prayer

God of peace, give a sense of hope to your people who live in countries experiencing conflict. Give wisdom to those in powerful positions to love and rule people with earnest love. May they receive the love and nourishment they deserve, and may they strengthen each other through the circumstances we cannot begin to imagine. Encourage those who work for peace, justice and reconciliation, give them understanding and patience and a resolve not to give up. Guard and guide us when we are weak and strengthen us in all adversity. May they know the love of Jesus Christ. *Amen.*

Amos 5:18-24

¹⁸Alas for you who desire the day of the LORD! Why do you want the day of the LORD? It is darkness, not light; ¹⁹as if someone fled from a lion, and was met by a bear; or went into the house and rested a hand against the wall, and was bitten by a snake. ²⁰Is not the day of the LORD darkness, not light, and gloom with no brightness in it?

²¹I hate, I despise your festivals, and I take no delight in your solemn assemblies. ²²Even though you offer me your burnt offerings and grain offerings, I will not accept them; and the offerings of well-being of your fatted animals I will not look upon. ²³Take away from me the noise of your songs; I will not listen to the melody of your harps. ²⁴But let justice roll down like waters, and righteousness like an everflowing stream.

Reflection

In 1963, Martin Luther King Jr. helped organize the March on Washington, D.C. A crowd of half a million people made on pilgrimage from all over the country to seek justice for black people. From the steps of the Lincoln Memorial, Dr. King quoted the prophet Amos, saying what has turned out to be the most meaningful and significant biblical text of my entire life: "But let justice roll down like waters, and righteousness like an ever-flowing stream."

I was born ten years after Dr. King's speech, spent time in biblical studies in seminary, studied social anthropology, and taught classes in different Christian seminaries. Yet Dr. King's words and those of Amos continued to chase me so that, to this very day, I remain strongly motivated to serve those in need.

Amos offers us a view of *mishpat* (justice), which has to do with right order in society, especially related to the poor and the weak, and *tzadeqah* (righteousness), which has to do with right relationships. This perspective led me to understand that if we are related to God, we have to care about the things that God cares about. Amos reminds us that God cares about the poor and disadvantaged, just as much as God cares about wholehearted worship.

Later, I realized that just as Dr. King embodied his struggle and his dream, with millions of eager faces seeking a genuine freedom, my dream also should have a specific face, a particular cause, something worthy of the efforts of a lifetime. After that personal insight, my women's rights advocacy began. Invited as a guest of the White House for a meeting of religious leaders in partnership with the United Nations Population Fund, I found myself almost in tears at the Lincoln Memorial. The words of the prophet Amos took on a very personal meaning. It was there where my own dream acquired the same passion that ignited Amos and Dr. King.

The Rev. Adrian Cardenas-Torres
Cathedral of Saint Luke
Republic of Panama

Questions:

What scripture verses help you identify those most vulnerable in your particular social context?

Knowing the powerful influence that can trigger the passion of a person moved by the Holy Spirit, what are the faces that appear in your dream of a more just and righteous society?

Prayer

Almighty God, you take no delight in a worship devoid of true love for our neighbors, especially those who are victims of injustice and marginalization: Grant that, following the example of your prophetic witnesses, we may be determined to work and fight until justice rolls down like waters, and righteousness like an ever-flowing stream; through Jesus Christ our Lord, who lives and reigns with you and the Holy Spirit, one God, for ever and ever. *Amen.*

Micah 6:1-16

6 Hear what the LORD says: Rise, plead your case before the mountains, and let the hills hear your voice. ²Hear, you mountains, the controversy of the LORD, and you enduring foundations of the earth; for the LORD has a controversy with his people, and he will contend with Israel.

³"O my people, what have I done to you? In what have I wearied you? Answer me! ⁴For I brought you up from the land of Egypt, and redeemed you from the house of slavery; and I sent before you Moses, Aaron, and Miriam. ⁵O my people, remember now what King Balak of Moab devised, what Balaam son of Beor answered him, and what happened from Shittim to Gilgal, that you may know the saving acts of the LORD."

⁶"With what shall I come before the LORD, and bow myself before God on high? Shall I come before him with burnt offerings, with calves a year old? ⁷Will the LORD be pleased with thousands of rams, with ten thousands of rivers of oil? Shall I give my firstborn for my transgression, the fruit of my body for the sin of my soul?" ⁸He has told you, O mortal, what is good; and what does the LORD require of you but to do justice, and to love kindness, and to walk humbly with your God?

⁹The voice of the LORD cries to the city (it is sound wisdom to fear your name): Hear, O tribe and assembly of the city! ¹⁰Can I forget the treasures of wickedness in the house of the wicked, and the scant measure that is accursed? ¹¹Can I tolerate wicked scales and a bag of dishonest weights? ¹²Your wealthy are full of violence; your inhabitants speak lies, with tongues of deceit

in their mouths. [13]Therefore I have begun to strike you down, making you desolate because of your sins. [14]You shall eat, but not be satisfied, and there shall be a gnawing hunger within you; you shall put away, but not save, and what you save, I will hand over to the sword. [15]You shall sow, but not reap; you shall tread olives, but not anoint yourselves with oil; you shall tread grapes, but not drink wine. [16]For you have kept the statutes of Omri and all the works of the house of Ahab, and you have followed their counsels. Therefore I will make you a desolation, and your inhabitants an object of hissing; so you shall bear the scorn of my people.

Reflection

I was born into a mixed-race family in the 1950s in a society still very much marked by colonial imperialism. Even as a child I knew how it felt to be considered less worthy, less attractive, less intelligent simply because of the color of my skin. My life was very much shaped and formed by the sharp sting of both attitudinal and structural injustice from a very early age.

Fortunately, I was born into an Indigenous family or *whanau* who were deeply involved in the struggle for Indigenous rights, especially halting land confiscations and preventing further loss of Indigenous language and culture.

The resilience, determination, and commitment to justice of my forebearers was deeply grounded in their faith in a missionary God of justice, of mercy, and of kindness.

In keeping with Indigenous tradition, my tribal elders sacrificed much in order that their chosen few could be well educated. They understood the political, social, and economic advantages of higher education—not just for the select individuals privileged by such opportunity but ultimately for the whole tribe, for whom their vision of release from colonial bondage was ultimately intended. I was incalculably blessed to have been chosen and set aside in this incredibly loving way.

In turn, one of their most loving and insistent teachings to me was always to remember the simple, yet profound words of Micah 6:8: "What does the LORD require of you but to do justice, and to love kindness, and to walk humbly with your God?"

In my work as a theology educator, a national and international church leader, chair of the Anglican Peace and Justice network, and as an advocate for Indigenous peoples, women, and human rights for all, these enduring words from Micah have unerringly informed my actions, words, and prayers.

Of very special importance to me has been my work alongside sisters and brothers in the Palestinian territories. In this contemporary circumstance of living under occupation, I have found deep resonance with the experience of my own people.

Through the horrors of colonization in Aotearoa, New Zealand, Maori people were often forcibly and brutally displaced from traditional lands, which had been in their care for centuries. In their stead came colonial occupiers who disenfranchised the original owners, not only of their land but also their precious cultural identity.

Thanks be to God, New Zealand Maori have managed to reclaim much of what was lost. Although there is still a chasm of difference in social, political, and economic capital between Maori and all other people in New Zealand, at least we enjoy the fundamental human rights of freedom to exist, to travel, to speak out, and to protest—unlike our Palestinian sisters and brothers.

Ever since I became intimately acquainted with the historical reality of what has been happening to Palestine and her people, I have felt an irresistible faith-based call to try to make things right for those who suffer cruelly and unjustly and to act always with an eye to Micah's unequivocal reminder and mandate.

Jenny Te Paa Daniel
Chair, Anglican Peace and Justice Network
Auckland, New Zealand

Questions

Are you aware of what happened in Palestine in 1948? If not, spend some time researching these events.

Are you aware of any local circumstance where indigenous peoples have been forcibly removed and/or relocated away from their original homelands?

Prayer

God of justice, mercy, and kindness, look down with love upon the Indigenous peoples of your blessed planet Earth. Remind us all of our blessed responsibility to be as sisters and brothers always in Christ, and that injustice anywhere and everywhere for any reason is not of your desire. Enable us to become courageous faith-filled advocates and exemplars of your peace with justice. *Amen.*

Matthew 11:1-6

11 Now when Jesus had finished instructing his twelve disciples, he went on from there to teach and proclaim his message in their cities.

²When John heard in prison what the Messiah was doing, he sent word by his disciples ³and said to him, "Are you the one who is to come, or are we to wait for another?" ⁴Jesus answered them, "Go and tell John what you hear and see: ⁵the blind receive their sight, the lame walk, the lepers are cleansed, the deaf hear, the dead are raised, and the poor have good news brought to them. ⁶And blessed is anyone who takes no offense at me."

Reflection

This passage has spoken to me many times over the forty years I have been associated with St. Stephen and the Incarnation Episcopal Church / San Esteban y la Encarnación Iglesia Episcopal, an inner-city parish in Washington, D.C.

We hear one the most painful questions asked in the New Testament. John the Baptizer cannot ask the question himself, because he is locked away in prison. So John must ask his question through his disciples, who carry to Jesus the question that is troubling John and then carrying the answer of Jesus back to the doomed prophet. It is safe to assume that neither John nor Jesus anticipates being able to talk to each other face to face again. Both know that John will never get out of there alive.

"Are you the one who is to come, or are we to wait for another?" The question startles us, especially coming from John, who had protested that Jesus ought to be baptizing him, instead of the other way around (Matthew 3:13-14). People who take up the prophetic mantle in the name of God and in service to the poor and powerless know about this experience of wondering whether anything ever really changes, whether their efforts will make any difference, and sometimes wondering: "Where is God, the advocate of the poor?"

St. Stephen's was the first racially integrated Episcopal parish in Washington. It offered its pulpit to the Black Panthers and to the Berrigan brothers and other protesters against the Vietnam War. Its rector was tried in ecclesiastical court for allowing one of the ordained women of the Philadelphia 11 to preside at Holy Eucharist.Its loaves and fishes program has fed thousands of people over the course of every weekend and holiday for decades. The church has been on the forefront of fair housing policy, donating a large part of its land so that low-income people could remain in the neighborhood; it has been an advocate for lesbian/gay/bisexual/transgender folks, stood up to drug dealers, supported the homeless and unemployed, and used its building to host other neighborhood and advocacy groups. We are now working to combine our English and Spanish congregations.

As a member of the clergy at St. Stephen, I have met many people who remind me of John and his question. I have asked a version of it myself. The hymn "There is a balm in Gilead" speaks of feeling discouraged that our work is in vain "but then the Holy Spirit revives our souls again."

We take turns being Jesus to each other's John, calling attention to God's actions as we see them: the blind see, the lame walk, lepers are cleansed, the deaf hear, the dead are raised. These things are all impossible for us, but nothing is too difficult for the Lord. Early church fathers and mothers speak of the Holy Eucharist as the medicine of immortality; I think it is the living Bread and Wine that keep people coming to this place.

The Rev. A. Katherine Grieb
Virginia Theological Seminary
Alexandria, Virgina

Questions

Was Martin Luther King Jr. right that the arc of the universe is long but that it tends toward justice, or was he whistling in the dark?

Are there activists you know who could use a word of encouragement from you?

Is burnout a problem in your community? How can we talk more openly about discouragement and despair in the context of Christian faith in God?

Prayer

Holy and gracious God, You are the One who creates and makes all things new: renew us in the power of your Holy Spirit. You are the One who taught us what love and faithfulness look like in the love of Jesus Christ who remained faithful even to death on the Cross: remind us of your love for all people and of your ability to bring resurrection life out of death. You are the One who saves and heals: hold our lives and the lives of all your people close to your heart, that we may be encouraged to work for justice and peace, to plant trees that we may never see, to continue to see visions and dream dreams that in your good time will come to pass. *Amen.*

Matthew 20:1–16

20 "For the kingdom of heaven is like a landowner who went out early in the morning to hire laborers for his vineyard. ²After agreeing with the laborers for the usual daily wage, he sent them into his vineyard. ³When he went out about nine o'clock, he saw others standing idle in the marketplace; ⁴and he said to them, 'You also go into the vineyard, and I will pay you whatever is right.' So they went. ⁵When he went out again about noon and about three o'clock, he did the same. ⁶And about five o'clock he went out and found others standing around; and he said to them, 'Why are you standing here idle all day?' ⁷They said to him, 'Because no one has hired us.' He said to them, 'You also go into the vineyard.' ⁸When evening came, the owner of the vineyard said to his manager, 'Call the laborers and give them their pay, beginning with the last and then going to the first.' ⁹When those hired about five o'clock came, each of them received the usual daily wage. ¹⁰Now when the first came, they thought they would receive more; but each of them also received the usual daily wage. ¹¹And when they received it, they grumbled against the landowner, ¹²saying, 'These last worked only one hour, and you have made them equal to us who have borne the burden of the day and the scorching heat.' ¹³But he replied to one of them, 'Friend, I am doing you no wrong; did you not agree with me for the usual daily wage? ¹⁴Take what belongs to you and go; I choose to give to this last the same as I give to you. ¹⁵Am I not allowed to do what I choose with what belongs to me? Or are you envious because I am generous?' ¹⁶So the last will be first, and the first will be last."

Reflection

A few blocks from my house, hundreds of day laborers gather before daybreak, waiting for someone to hire them for hard work. Sometimes I see a crowd around a guy in a truck who's pointing and picking: this one, this one, that one. There's a smaller group of workers at noon, still flagging down drivers, hoping to be hired for half a day. And in the late afternoon a dozen men still wait for the chance of a last-minute job.

As in Jesus' time, the economy of the world governs who's hired. The first picks are the strongest-looking, cleverest younger workers; at noon are the ones who are energetic and speak some English; late in the afternoon, the ones who speak only Spanish. And finally just the smaller, older men—along with the lame and simple-minded––are left to wait, unpaid, as the hours pass.

But something else happens on that street corner: Every day, neighborhood church women rise early and bring pan dulce and hot coffee to the laborers. They don't offer free breakfast to the strongest first or hand it only to the smart, good-looking young ones. They give it to the lazy drunks. To the old man with a bad knee. To losers. The women push carts loaded with enough food for everyone, and they offer it indiscriminately.

The kingdom of heaven, Jesus says, is like this: God is not fair but merciful. We can't keep God from being generous to others. First or last, early-bird or slacker, God offers each of us work in the kingdom, feeding us all from an overflowing cart, no matter what any of us actually "deserve."

God knows the world isn't fair. I'm paid to sit indoors and write while another woman works at the carwash, shivering in wet clothes for ten hours a day. For being born white, I'm mostly first, while others with darker skin are forced to be last. And if scripture means anything, it is that we are responsible for making the world more just—especially those, like me, who benefit from the unfairness of privilege.

But it is God's pleasure to freely give everybody what nobody can earn. So while we strive to do justice in the world, let us labor with thanksgiving in the extravagant unfairness of the kingdom.

Sara Miles
The Food Pantry
St. Gregory of Nyssa Episcopal Church
San Francisco, California

Questions

What have you received that you haven't deserved?

When have you acted with mercy rather than fairness?

Prayer

Gracious God, who sent your son to eat with sinners and love the undeserving: you give us what we can never earn. Open our hearts to fully receive your mercy, that we might be merciful, and live in the generosity of your kingdom, through Jesus Christ our Lord. *Amen*.

Matthew 21:12-16

¹²Then Jesus entered the temple and drove out all who were selling and buying in the temple, and he overturned the tables of the money changers and the seats of those who sold doves. ¹³He said to them, "It is written, 'My house shall be called a house of prayer'; but you are making it a den of robbers."

¹⁴The blind and the lame came to him in the temple, and he cured them. ¹⁵But when the chief priests and the scribes saw the amazing things that he did, and heard the children crying out in the temple, "Hosanna to the Son of David," they became angry ¹⁶and said to him, "Do you hear what these are saying?" Jesus said to them, "Yes; have you never read, 'Out of the mouths of infants and nursing babies you have prepared praise for yourself'?"

Reflection

In the socio-cultural context of Jesus, children have no social value. They are not even counted in the statistics. In the contemporary world that we call civilized, the rights of children and adolescents are still very fragile, with countless forms of violence perpetrated against them around the world.

Jesus enters the temple knowing that this sacred space is used and manipulated for lucrative businesses, where dirty money operates with a legal facade justified by the fulfillment and performance of religious rites. Moneychangers, vendors, racketeers, blackmailers, swindlers, and greedy persons roam freely in the shadow of the temple.

Matthew tells us that Jesus is indignant and takes action against the merchants. Jesus reaches out to the outcasts, the blind, the lame, the sick, and all those who need his healing and liberating touch. What is significant is that they come with children singing praises. That sacred space opens itself to the most valuable asset of any society and culture—younger generations who can be integrated as active members of the liberating power of Jesus.

With scorn and anger the chief priests ask, "Do you hear what the people are saying?" Jesus responds with the words of Psalm 8:2, giving recognition to the dignity of human beings from their first days of life, emphasizing the innate value among younger generations.

This passage has deep meaning for today as millions of boys and girls experience abuses of every kind and at all levels. They suffer from hunger, neglect, sexual exploitation, drugs, wars, evictions, and many other kinds of mistreatment, including physical abuse, alienation, loneliness, excessive abuse of the Internet, exacerbated consumerism, family neglect, and emotional and spiritual impairment.

In the maelstrom of today's world, this demeaning and unfair situation cannot be overlooked. The desperate cry of children is barely heard. Their lives are fragile, and their future as adults is uncertain. The gospel says, however, that they are co-sharers with Jesus in his restorative justice and action; they will make their voices heard, and they will make the hearts of the unjust tremble.

Jesus disturbs us. Jesus demands: Woe to us if we allow any of these little ones to perish! Jesus calls us to care for the children and to be like them, to be simple and sincere, to internalize the kingdom of God and his righteousness.

The Rt. Rev. Maria Griselda Delgado del Carpio
Episcopal Church of Cuba
Havana, Cuba

Questions

Do you know children living in adverse situations? What are the biggest challenges for them and for you?

What situations exist in other contexts where you can get involved on behalf of children or adolescents?

The gospel calls us to work for justice and the integrity of every human being. What is our responsibility to younger generations?

Prayer

Creator God, you made us in your image and likeness, in goodness, solidarity and deep love, for which we offer our gratitude. We lift up to you all children and young people living in extreme situations. Forgive us for having lukewarm hearts, and give us courage to face heartbreaking and harrowing situations experienced by children and youth. Give us a clear vision to work for justice for every child and youth around us so that we can discover the wonders of your healing and liberating gospel. May the Holy Spirit guide our steps today and forever. *Amen.*

Matthew 25:31-46

[31]"When the Son of Man comes in his glory, and all the angels with him, then he will sit on the throne of his glory. [32]All the nations will be gathered before him, and he will separate people one from another as a shepherd separates the sheep from the goats, [33]and he will put the sheep at his right hand and the goats at the left. [34]Then the king will say to those at his right hand, 'Come, you that are blessed by my Father, inherit the kingdom prepared for you from the foundation of the world; [35]for I was hungry and you gave me food, I was thirsty and you gave me something to drink, I was a stranger and you welcomed me, [36]I was naked and you gave me clothing, I was sick and you took care of me, I was in prison and you visited me.' [37]Then the righteous will answer him, 'Lord, when was it that we saw you hungry and gave you food, or thirsty and gave you something to drink? [38]And when was it that we saw you a stranger and welcomed you, or naked and gave you clothing? [39]And when was it that we saw you sick or in prison and visited you?' [40]And the king will answer them, 'Truly I tell you, just as you did it to one of the least of these who are members of my family, you did it to me.' [41]Then he will say to those at his left hand, 'You that are accursed, depart from me into the eternal fire prepared for the devil and his angels; [42]for I was hungry and you gave me no food, I was thirsty and you gave me nothing to drink, [43]I was a stranger and you did not welcome me, naked and you did not give me clothing, sick and in prison and you did not visit me.' [44]Then they also will answer, 'Lord, when was it that we saw you hungry or thirsty

or a stranger or naked or sick or in prison, and did not take care of you?' ⁴⁵Then he will answer them, 'Truly I tell you, just as you did not do it to one of the least of these, you did not do it to me.' ⁴⁶And these will go away into eternal punishment, but the righteous into eternal life."

Reflection

These days, millions of people have taken to the road, looking for a future for themselves and their families. Of the 6.5 million Syrian refugees, Jordan has accepted some 1.25 million, and Germany has taken in another million or more. Large numbers of refugees are in Lebanon and Turkey, and thousands are scattered around the globe.

War, poverty, hunger, sickness, and the dream of a better life drive them. They cross cold and dangerous seas and walk thousands of miles, braving hunger and thirst, humiliation and exploitation. Children, uprooted and torn from their families, are sent by despairing fathers and mothers with tears in their eyes and prayers in their hearts. Thank God for the goodness and kindnesses they meet along the way, just like Mary and Joseph did in Bethlehem. Thank God that we here in Jordan are able to pick up some of the pieces of their shattered lives and look after their disabled children.

These refugees remind us that many of us—now their hosts—were once uninvited guests ourselves, separated from family and community, fleeing catastrophe and death, looking for a future for our families and children, praying to survive till tomorrow.

Inevitably there are terrorists, not unlike the murdering soldiers of King Herod, following or hiding among them. But among those thousands of people who are our uninvited guests will be many who came especially to be a blessing to us as well, bringing us our inheritance of the kingdom. They follow in the footsteps of Joseph and Mary, the shepherds, the wise men and the angels—and above all, the child Jesus. Perhaps, as it is written, by giving hospitality we harbor angels, and we cherish, nourish, and welcome a king. When Jesus speaks of the uninvited guests in the Gospel of Matthew, he may be remembering what Mary must have told him about their frantic flight to Egypt. The Messiah, the Christ, became a refugee—an uninvited guest himself—but not to seek a better life. He came to give it.

The Rev. Canon Brother Andrew A.L. de Carpentier
Holy Land Institute for Deaf and Deafblind Children
Salt, Jordan

Questions

How often do we see refugees as God's special envoys, his ambassadors, who present us with our inheritance—the kingdom of our Lord?

We mostly think of Jesus as our invited guest. After all, we invite him into our lives. How often do you think Jesus sees himself as a refugee searching for a place to stay, much as he describes himself in the Gospel of Matthew?

The Social Justice Bible Challenge

Prayer

Dear Lord, we remember the women of Jerusalem who quenched your thirst; Joseph of Arimathea who shared with you his grave. Help us to be among those who bring you comfort and clothing, food, water, and home. Give us hearts that are open and the grace to treat all people with dignity and love. *Amen.*

Mark 6:30-44

[30]The apostles gathered around Jesus, and told him all that they had done and taught. [31]He said to them, "Come away to a deserted place all by yourselves and rest a while." For many were coming and going, and they had no leisure even to eat. [32]And they went away in the boat to a deserted place by themselves. [33]Now many saw them going and recognized them, and they hurried there on foot from all the towns and arrived ahead of them. [34]As he went ashore, he saw a great crowd; and he had compassion for them, because they were like sheep without a shepherd; and he began to teach them many things. [35]When it grew late, his disciples came to him and said, "This is a deserted place, and the hour is now very late; [36]send them away so that they may go into the surrounding country and villages and buy something for themselves to eat." [37]But he answered them, "You give them something to eat." They said to him, "Are we to go and buy two hundred denarii worth of bread, and give it to them to eat?" [38]And he said to them, "How many loaves have you? Go and see." When they had found out, they said, "Five, and two fish." [39]Then he ordered them to get all the people to sit down in groups on the green grass. [40]So they sat down in groups of hundreds and of fifties. [41]Taking the five loaves and the two fish, he looked up to heaven, and blessed and broke the loaves, and gave them to his disciples to set before the people; and he divided the two fish among them all. [42]And all ate and were filled; [43]and they took up twelve baskets full of broken pieces and of the fish. [44]Those who had eaten the loaves numbered five thousand men.

Reflection

As we implement programs in southern Africa aimed at poverty eradication, social development, and economic justice, the story of the feeding of the five thousand is often used to illustrate the immense benefit and positive result that can be achieved when we have faith, believing that the resources provided by God are enough, even more than enough to meet all our needs.

The story resonates with all of us involved in community development: We, like the disciples, get tired and need a break. Jesus recognizes that the disciples are worn out and need some time to be refreshed, renewed, and rejuvenated. Such acts of self-care are often interrupted by the very real cry of people who are in need and who seek hope.

When Jesus sees the crowds, the texts say that he has compassion on them. Compassion compels Jesus to minister to the crowd, as he understands their plight as a people needing hope and leadership. Compassion is not simply about feeling pity for the other; it is rooted in alleviating the suffering of the other.

The disciples, in their tired states, are most likely disappointed by not having time alone with Jesus to rest, but over and above that, they predict a crisis: Everyone will be getting hungry, and they are not in a place where food can easily be found. What is even more daunting for the disciples is that Jesus expects them to feed the people!

Often we face what seem to be insurmountable challenges, and we simply do not have enough money or human power to solve the problems.

Jesus illustrates that people are not without solutions themselves. All people have something to offer that, when combined with the skills and resources of others, multiplies to provide abundantly for all.

Canon Delene Mark
HOPE Africa
Anglican Church of Southern Africa

Questions

In a modern-day setting, how do non-profit agencies and churches deal with 5,000 hungry men, plus women and children, in isolated places?

How can we change our outreach ministries to display the true qualities of compassion?

Prayer

O God our creator, sustainer and redeemer: We pray for a world where people are willing to share everything to benefit humanity. Help us strive for justice and equity, recognizing the immense wealth present in our midst. May we always act in faith, believing that you equip us for the insurmountable. *Amen.*

Mark 10:13-16

[13]People were bringing little children to him in order that he might touch them; and the disciples spoke sternly to them. [14]But when Jesus saw this, he was indignant and said to them, "Let the little children come to me; do not stop them; for it is to such as these that the kingdom of God belongs. [15]Truly I tell you, whoever does not receive the kingdom of God as a little child will never enter it." [16]And he took them up in his arms, laid his hands on them, and blessed them.

Reflection

Perhaps Jesus' followers are exasperated by the pesky presence of little ones under their feet, the constant demands of their physical and emotional needs, or even their nettlesome questions, asking "Why?" Or maybe it was just the end of a long workday, and they are tired so they push these innocent ones away. Whatever the reason, Jesus' retort is swift and to the point. Moreover, his actions are as concrete and steadfast as his words.

We can neither receive nor build, let alone find, that for which we are looking if we cannot welcome and accept into our arms the children of this world and protect them, nourish them, encourage and love them—for to such belongs the kingdom of God.

It seems rare for a child to overlook injustice or miss a moment to identify adult hypocrisy—a condition too often excused by the well-repeated maxim, "Do as I say, not as I do." And in the consumer-driven materialism that fuels our modern economy, there is a tendency to overlook injustices toward children even when we know better.

Worldwide, 3.5 million children die each year because of starvation. In the United States, one in five children go to bed hungry. Our country's once-proud public education system, with promises not just of sound education but of civic engagement, is eroding. Human trafficking of children continues. Kids toil in sweatshops, making our clothes and sneakers. They endure long days in the fields pulling in our crops. They are victimized in more ways than we care to know about or acknowledge.

"Of course," we say, "these are not *our* kids. We watch out for them!" But did Jesus ever say our neighbor's children should be treated or loved differently than our own?

The Rev. Edmund K. "Ned" Sherrill II
Church Farm School
Exton, Pennsylvania

Questions_____

What kind of cultural seeds are we sowing if one in five children go to bed hungry, even in the most affluent areas of American society?

How are the children in and around our faith communities truly received, blessed, protected, and nurtured by them?

What child-like spirit do you hope to maintain in your journey toward God's kingdom?

Prayer _____

O God, you welcome children into your arms to build the kingdom: Strengthen and guide people of all ages through the struggles, confusion, and silent indifference we harbor so that we may gain a deeper knowledge of your presence and promise in the face of all children. In Christ's name we pray. *Amen.*

Mark 10:17-31

[17]As he was setting out on a journey, a man ran up and knelt before him, and asked him, "Good Teacher, what must I do to inherit eternal life?" [18]Jesus said to him, "Why do you call me good? No one is good but God alone. [19]You know the commandments: 'You shall not murder; You shall not commit adultery; You shall not steal; You shall not bear false witness; You shall not defraud; Honor your father and mother.'" [20]He said to him, "Teacher, I have kept all these since my youth." [21]Jesus, looking at him, loved him and said, "You lack one thing; go, sell what you own, and give the money to the poor, and you will have treasure in heaven; then come, follow me." [22]When he heard this, he was shocked and went away grieving, for he had many possessions.

[23]Then Jesus looked around and said to his disciples, "How hard it will be for those who have wealth to enter the kingdom of God!" [24]And the disciples were perplexed at these words. But Jesus said to them again, "Children, how hard it is to enter the kingdom of God! [25]It is easier for a camel to go through the eye of a needle than for someone who is rich to enter the kingdom of God." [26]They were greatly astounded and said to one another, "Then who can be saved?" [27]Jesus looked at them and said, "For mortals it is impossible, but not for God; for God all things are possible."

[28]Peter began to say to him, "Look, we have left everything and followed you." [29]Jesus said, "Truly I tell you, there is no one who has left house or brothers or sisters or mother or father or

children or fields, for my sake and for the sake of the good news, ³⁰who will not receive a hundredfold now in this age—houses, brothers and sisters, mothers and children, and fields with persecutions—and in the age to come eternal life. ³¹But many who are first will be last, and the last will be first."

Reflection

Two concerns appear often in scripture: How do we enter the kingdom of God and what must we do to inherit eternal life? Jesus declares that the kingdom of God is at hand, and we proclaim at the Holy Eucharist that the body of Christ and the cup of salvation "keep us in eternal life." Yet we continue to focus our concerns on what happens to us after we leave this mortal existence.

Mark's tenth chapter is revolutionary, from Jesus' response regarding marriage, divorce, and the nature of children to how one obtains eternal life.

When asked by someone on the threshold of a potentially perilous journey, Jesus declares that only God is good. This is the only reference I know of where Jesus challenges the subsequent theological dogma that he was "without sin" and therefore sinless.

Jesus accepts this person's declaration of having faithfully kept all the commandments and then "Jesus, looking at him, loved him and said, 'You lack one thing; go, sell what you own, and give the money to the poor, and you will have treasure in heaven; then come, follow me.'"

And the man went away grieving, for he had many possessions.

In our present world of have-and-have-nots, we need to ask ourselves whether we are a reflection of our possessions or whether our possessions possess us. Can we sell what has us and become free of our bondage to the illusion of ownership and possessions so that we might follow Jesus' way and allow creation's abundance to reach all God's children?

The belief in Jesus' day that wealth was confirmation of being saved is turned upside-down in this episode, and it stuns the disciples.

Yet, Jesus reassures those who would hear that anyone who leaves these many things—family, work, and possessions—for Jesus' sake and the sake of the gospel will receive back a hundred-fold in this life…and in the age to come, eternal life.

Dr. H.M. McFarling III
Atlanta Obstetrics and Gynecology Associates
Atlanta, Georgia

Questions

How does our accumulation and clinging to possessions contribute to poverty?

How does our notion of the kingdom to come in the next life contribute to social injustice in our present life as nations and religions?

Prayer

Almighty God, we invite you to help us to give away more of what we have and to share more freely our time, expertise, and energy so that we might bring your life-giving gospel to earth in this life, as we await the age to come. *Amen.*

Mark 10:46-52

⁴⁶They came to Jericho. As he and his disciples and a large crowd were leaving Jericho, Bartimaeus son of Timaeus, a blind beggar, was sitting by the roadside. ⁴⁷When he heard that it was Jesus of Nazareth, he began to shout out and say, "Jesus, Son of David, have mercy on me!" ⁴⁸Many sternly ordered him to be quiet, but he cried out even more loudly, "Son of David, have mercy on me!" ⁴⁹Jesus stood still and said, "Call him here." And they called the blind man, saying to him, "Take heart; get up, he is calling you." ⁵⁰So throwing off his cloak, he sprang up and came to Jesus. ⁵¹Then Jesus said to him, "What do you want me to do for you?" The blind man said to him, "My teacher, let me see again." ⁵²Jesus said to him, "Go; your faith has made you well." Immediately he regained his sight and followed him on the way.

Reflection

When I began my ministry at a church in West Harlem, I met some of the most generous people I have ever known. Potlucks at city churches are tricky, with most folks arriving with something to unwrap from a deli. But our going-away party from St. Mary's was the mother of all potlucks, featuring a cast-iron skillet casserole filled with Enita

Hinkson's prized curried goat. Enita had spent two days preparing her family specialty, beginning at a live meat market.

The story of Bartimeaus speaks volumes to me about what matters in ministry. It starts with a lone beggar by the side of the road, a common sight in New York today. Bartimaeus sits in his cloak, his major material possession. He is clearly dependent, but just because he is destitute and blind does not mean he is not capable. In fact, he is keenly observing the world around him. Understanding at once who is coming, Bartimaeus refuses to be quieted and engages Jesus' attention. His passion is so strong that he throws aside his cloak and leaps toward Jesus with a bold request: "My teacher, let me see again." Despite his blindness, he recognizes Jesus, while those with sight do not.

To understand an alternative to Bartimaeus's witness, look back to the rich young man in Mark 10:10-22. His request is to inherit eternal life. When Jesus reminds the man about the importance of keeping the commandments, the man astonishingly replies that he has kept them all since his youth. Jesus' look uniquely affirms this claim. But then Jesus directs the man to give away all that he has, and the man "was shocked and went away grieving."

So what should I pay attention to? What do I value? Bartimeaus leaves behind his sole possession of a cloak, while the prosperous young man who zealously keeps God's law is trapped by his wealth. Jesus sees them both as God sees them. For me, these two encounters define discipleship and what it means to live trusting the Spirit, which is the challenge of my ministry, with many thanks to Enita and Jesus for their nourishment and love.

The Rev. Canon Jamie Callaway
Colleges and Universities of the Anglican Communion
New York City, New York

Questions

The recent wave of refugees is one of the world's most explosive social issues. There are now 100 million refugees, representing one percent of the world's population. What does Jesus' encounter with Bartimaeus and the rich man say about how we see and respond to refugees?

Who has helped shape your ministry? What difference has this person made in your life?

Prayer

God of compassion, enable us to see the world through your loving eyes, so that we may always be ready to live our faith and love our neighbors as you love both them and us. Guide us, Jesus our shepherd, along the way, and may the Holy Spirit live and reign within us now and for ever. *Amen.*

Luke 1:39-55

[39]In those days Mary set out and went with haste to a Judean town in the hill country, [40]where she entered the house of Zechariah and greeted Elizabeth. [41]When Elizabeth heard Mary's greeting, the child leaped in her womb. And Elizabeth was filled with the Holy Spirit [42]and exclaimed with a loud cry, "Blessed are you among women, and blessed is the fruit of your womb. [43]And why has this happened to me, that the mother of my Lord comes to me? [44]For as soon as I heard the sound of your greeting, the child in my womb leaped for joy. [45]And blessed is she who believed that there would be a fulfillment of what was spoken to her by the Lord." [46]And Mary said, "My soul magnifies the Lord, [47]and my spirit rejoices in God my Savior, [48]for he has looked with favor on the lowliness of his servant. Surely, from now on all generations will call me blessed; [49]for the Mighty One has done great things for me, and holy is his name. [50]His mercy is for those who fear him from generation to generation. [51]He has shown strength with his arm; he has scattered the proud in the thoughts of their hearts. [52]He has brought down the powerful from their thrones, and lifted up the lowly; [53]he has filled the hungry with good things, and sent the rich away empty. [54]He has helped his servant Israel, in remembrance of his mercy, [55]according to the promise he made to our ancestors, to Abraham and to his descendants forever."

Reflection

Mary, Mother of God, is often called meek and mild. But in this reading, she is impulsive, brave, and radical. Having been told by the archangel that she will become the mother of the Son of God, Mary takes off. She travels alone 100 miles to visit her elderly cousin Elizabeth. When Mary sees that her cousin is also pregnant, as the angel has said, she realizes that she—a young girl of no wealth or status—is to be the mother of the Christ. And so she lifts up her voice to sing her song of joy.

Mary praises God and then goes on to say things about God that are as shocking today as they were 2,000 years ago. God has scattered the proud, brought down the powerful, and lifted up the lowly. God has fed the hungry with good things and sent the rich away empty. Mary sings that God is not only lifting up the poor but also that God is tearing the powerful and the rich down from lofty places. This is radical indeed, particularly in our time in which the wealthy are honored and emulated. Mary understands that poor and vulnerable know that they need God's provision and mercy. Wealthy and powerful people often suffer under the delusion that they are enough in themselves.

I find this feisty, outspoken Mary inspiring and challenging. This young woman sees the true nature of God through her humility and courage and is chosen to be the means by which Jesus the Christ comes into the world. We too, are called to bring Christ into the world by being humble, trusting, and brave, just like Mary. This reading calls us out of our power and into the emptiness that only God can fill.

The Ven. Dr. Pamela M. Nesbit
Episcopal Diocese of Pennsylvania
Philadelphia, Pennsylvania

Questions

How do you feel about what Mary is saying about God's relationship with the rich and the poor? Are you comfortable with it?

What changes does this reading invite you to consider in your own life?

Prayer

Loving God, you called our mother Mary to become the means by which our Lord Jesus Christ came into the world: Help us to so trust you that we might let go of everything that keeps us from bringing Christ's love into the world. *Amen.*

Luke 4:16-19

¹⁶When he came to Nazareth, where he had been brought up, he went to the synagogue on the sabbath day, as was his custom. He stood up to read, ¹⁷and the scroll of the prophet Isaiah was given to him. He unrolled the scroll and found the place where it was written:

¹⁸"The Spirit of the Lord is upon me, because he has anointed me to bring good news to the poor. He has sent me to proclaim release to the captives and recovery of sight to the blind, to let the oppressed go free, ¹⁹to proclaim the year of the Lord's favor."

Reflection

How is it possible to be black and Christian? This question was paramount to me as I entered the process for ordained ministry in 1968. This soul-searching and ponderous issue had its origins during the antebellum period when black clergy, slaves, and emancipated individuals tried to reconcile the reality of their oppressed conditions with the professed Christianity of their present and former masters.

On one occasion African American Episcopal (A.M.E.) Church Bishop Daniel Payne asked a slave if he were a Christian. The slave replied, "No sir, white men treat us so bad in Mississippi that we can't be Christians." Reflecting on this issue from his personal experience,

Bishop Payne declared in 1852: "Sometimes it seemed as though some wild beast had plunged his fangs into my heart, and was squeezing out its life-blood. Then I began to question the existence of God, and to say if he does exist, is he just? If so, why does he suffer one race to oppress and enslave another, to rob them by unrighteous enactments of rights, which they hold most dear and sacred? Sometimes I wished for the lawmakers what Nero wished, that the Romans had but one neck. I would be the man to sever the head from its shoulders. Again said I: Is there no God?"

Many mid-1960s civil rights activists concluded that it wasn't possible to be black and Christian. As one who was engaged in social activism, my answer to this question was foundational to my decision to enter the ministry.

Ultimately I turned to the Bible to inform my answer. After a great deal of reflection and prayer, I concluded that it is possible to be black and Christian. Reading certain scriptures from the perspective of a historically marginalized person, I learned that the God of the Judeo-Christian tradition chose to make himself known in history by identifying with a band of oppressed slaves in North Africa and in Egypt. In order that no one would misunderstand that he had come to proclaim liberation to the oppressed, Jesus enters into the temple, the center of Jewish life, and defines the nature of his ministry by reading from the words of Isaiah. The liberation that Jesus proclaims is one of mind, body, and soul. He dedicates his life to this liberation and ultimately gives his life for the cause of liberating people from the forces that prevent us from being the person God intends.

The Christ event today is a liberation—taking place wherever men and women, boys and girls, who are oppressed in mind, body, or spirit, are seeking to free themselves of the forces that bind them. Questioning and skeptical brothers and sisters will only know of the liberating power of Jesus Christ by what they see and hear from Christians who seek to be agents of Christ's liberating power in this world. The actions of professed believers in the saving power of Jesus Christ hold the answer as to whether or not it is, indeed, possible to be black and Christian.

The Rev. Richard L. Tolliver
St. Edmund's Episcopal Church
Chicago, Illinois

Questions _____

Has any issue ever caused you to question whether it's possible for you to be a Christian? If so, how did you resolve the issue?

How have you sought to be an agent of Christ's liberating ministry?

What is your hope for twenty-first century Christianity?

Prayer

O God, strengthen our resolve to manifest Christ's liberating message to those who feel oppressed in mind, body, and spirit and to those representatives of power structures who tacitly or willingly marginalize people. Reaffirm our commitment to good and right actions that manifest the kingdom of God on earth. Forgive us when we vacillate and fall short, causing us to be perceived as enemies of human liberation and justice. Out of evil, bring good, and make us strong as we seek to be witnesses to your love. *Amen.*

Luke 5:9-11

⁹For he and all who were with him were amazed at the catch of fish that they had taken; ¹⁰and so also were James and John, sons of Zebedee, who were partners with Simon. Then Jesus said to Simon, "Do not be afraid; from now on you will be catching people." ¹¹When they had brought their boats to shore, they left everything and followed him.

Reflection

All four gospels often quote Jesus as saying something along the lines of "Do not be afraid." I've heard it's the phrase used most often in the New Testament—and well it should be.

My job is working with churches and individuals to help them follow their call from God into the world. It's amazing to see the varied ways and places God calls us to connect with one another. There is no shortage of life-altering calls to be Jesus' hands and feet in the world, but fear often keeps us from saying "Yes." I've worked with numerous churches and individuals who feel in their souls true calls from God, but they are hesitant to follow because they are afraid. They push back, saying that answering the call would be too hard, too dangerous, too expensive, or too much out of their comfort zone.

We often hear that the opposite of faith isn't disbelief but rather fear. I've witnessed countless times the fact that when people overcome their fears and follow their calls, they are able to do things they never thought were possible. They engage in God's mission to the world in ways that forever transform them. They become fully alive, living into their God-given purposes.

Perhaps Jesus tells us so often in the gospels to "fear not" because he knows that what he is asking of us is truly scary. Like Simon, we are called to leave everything and follow Jesus, expected to work for social justice and peace—even when it's hard. We need to take risks—and take a stand. All that can be truly frightening, but we have God to walk along with us, calming our fears and assuring us that the kingdom is at hand.

Charles (Buck) Blanchard
Diocese of Virginia
Richmond, Virginia

Questions _____

Have you ever felt called by God to engage in mission to the world but did not follow through because of fear?

How can we support one another in community so that we all say "Yes" to our call from God?

Prayer _____

Good and gracious God, grant us the vison to see thy way, the grace to understand thy way, and the power to do thy way, all with humility. *Amen.*

Luke 7:36-50

³⁶One of the Pharisees asked Jesus to eat with him, and he went into the Pharisee's house and took his place at the table. ³⁷And a woman in the city, who was a sinner, having learned that he was eating in the Pharisee's house, brought an alabaster jar of ointment. ³⁸She stood behind him at his feet, weeping, and began to bathe his feet with her tears and to dry them with her hair. Then she continued kissing his feet and anointing them with the ointment. ³⁹Now when the Pharisee who had invited him saw it, he said to himself, "If this man were a prophet, he would have known who and what kind of woman this is who is touching him—that she is a sinner." ⁴⁰Jesus spoke up and said to him, "Simon, I have something to say to you." "Teacher," he replied, "Speak." ⁴¹"A certain creditor had two debtors; one owed five hundred denarii, and the other fifty. ⁴²When they could not pay, he canceled the debts for both of them. Now which of them will love him more?" ⁴³Simon answered, "I suppose the one for whom he canceled the greater debt." And Jesus said to him, "You have judged rightly." ⁴⁴Then turning toward the woman, he said to Simon, "Do you see this woman? I entered your house; you gave me no water for my feet, but she has bathed my feet with her tears and dried them with her hair. ⁴⁵You gave me no kiss, but from the time I came in she has not stopped kissing my feet. ⁴⁶You did not anoint my head with oil, but she has anointed my feet with ointment. ⁴⁷Therefore, I tell you, her sins, which were many, have been forgiven; hence she has shown great love. But the one to whom little is forgiven, loves little." ⁴⁸Then he said to

her, "Your sins are forgiven." [49]But those who were at the table with him began to say among themselves, "Who is this who even forgives sins?" [50]And he said to the woman, "Your faith has saved you; go in peace."

Reflection

Jesus is dining at the home of Simon, a Pharisee. A woman, "who was a sinner," enters the house and makes her way to Jesus. She washes his feet with her tears and anoints them with precious oil. We are not told why she carries this reputation as a sinner, as this category was quite broad in Jesus' day. Nor are we told why she is weeping. Could her tears be a sign of contrition or remorse for choices she has made (or been forced to make for social or economic reasons)? Could they be tears of gratitude? Is it possible that in her previous encounter(s) with Jesus, she has been treated with unexpected dignity and respect? Perhaps she has been forgiven by Jesus or healed. We do not know.

What is clear is that she is an unwelcomed guest. Simon objects to her presence and to Jesus' interaction with her. Simon's strict adherence to widely-accepted religious purity codes dictates his response to this woman. He knows better than to speak to her or allow her to touch him, and he assumes that Jesus knows this too.

Jesus asks Simon a startling question: "Do you see this woman?" Of course, Simon sees her. From the moment she enters the room, he is aware of her presence. Jesus is asking him something else. He wants to know if Simon can see her as she is, or if he is blinded by the label he has affixed to her. Jesus points out to him—and to each of us—all that he has missed about this woman, noting her kindness, generosity, and love.

Br. David Vryhof
Society of Saint John the Evangelist
Cambridge, Massachusettes

Questions _____

How often do we fail to see others, or to rightly understand their desires or needs, because we see a label instead of a person?

Is there a specific person or group of people whom you find it difficult to see without labeling? Can you take a fresh look at them, trying to see them as Jesus sees them?

What labels have you imposed on yourself that limit your ability to see yourself with Christ's eyes?

Prayer _____

Gracious God, who has bestowed dignity on every human being by creating us in your likeness: Grant us the grace to see one another and ourselves without labeling, judging, or blaming, so that we may recognize the wonder and mystery of human life, and glorify you, the giver of all. *Amen.*

Luke 10:25-37

²⁵Just then a lawyer stood up to test Jesus. "Teacher," he said, "what must I do to inherit eternal life?" ²⁶He said to him, "What is written in the law? What do you read there?" ²⁷He answered, "You shall love the Lord your God with all your heart, and with all your soul, and with all your strength, and with all your mind; and your neighbor as yourself." ²⁸And he said to him, "You have given the right answer; do this, and you will live."

²⁹But wanting to justify himself, he asked Jesus, "And who is my neighbor?" ³⁰Jesus replied, "A man was going down from Jerusalem to Jericho, and fell into the hands of robbers, who stripped him, beat him, and went away, leaving him half dead. ³¹Now by chance a priest was going down that road; and when he saw him, he passed by on the other side. ³²So likewise a Levite, when he came to the place and saw him, passed by on the other side. ³³But a Samaritan while traveling came near him; and when he saw him, he was moved with pity. ³⁴He went to him and bandaged his wounds, having poured oil and wine on them. Then he put him on his own animal, brought him to an inn, and took care of him. ³⁵The next day he took out two denarii, gave them to the innkeeper, and said, 'Take care of him; and when I come back, I will repay you whatever more you spend.' ³⁶Which of these three, do you think, was a neighbor to the man who fell into the hands of the robbers?" ³⁷He said, "The one who showed him mercy." Jesus said to him, "Go and do likewise."

Reflection

"And who is my neighbor?"

A simple question. And yet for the lawyer who tests Jesus, and for many of us, the answer is never simple. The one most different from the wounded man shows him mercy, while the most prominent members of his community fail to do so. I wince at the difficulty the lawyer has in even acknowledging the Samaritan, referring to the man as "the one who showed him mercy." His failure to see their human connection threatens to keep the lawyer from the fullness of the eternal life he seeks. Jesus invites this man—and you and me—into a broader vision of community, responsibility, and identity.

Today, it remains difficult to acknowledge that the neighbors we are commanded to love as ourselves come from different countries, profess different religions, and can present challenges to our understanding of morality.

I live and work in Rome, Italy, a city and nation at the nexus of the global refugee crisis. As droves of asylum seekers reach the Italian shores in battered boats, European Union policy makers and everyday citizens struggle to respond. Are these desperate, predominantly Muslim refugees our neighbors? What does it mean to show them mercy? The Joel Nafuma Refugee Center is one of the ways our church has chosen to respond.

The question of "Who is my neighbor?" is larger than this crisis. I submit that our answer determines how much we experience the promise of eternal life in the here and now. If we, like the lawyer, believe that our love and mercy should be directed only inward—toward members of our own tribe and only those who share our beliefs—then we experience isolation more hellish than heavenly. If, on the other hand, we recognize that God's mercy flows across all divides, we more readily become good neighbors and pass over the stumbling block of divisions in order to extend the mercy we have received freely and widely to all.

The Rev. Austin K. Rios
St. Paul's Within the Walls Episcopal Church
Rome, Italy

Questions

Who is hardest for you to see and treat as a neighbor? Why?

Have you shown mercy to someone who didn't expect to receive it from you? Have you ever been the recipient of unexpected mercy? What was the experience like in both cases?

How can you be a better neighbor?

Prayer

Loving God: May love flow freely from me, and may I receive love freely.

Merciful God: May mercy flow freely from me, and may I receive mercy freely.

Gracious God: May grace flow freely from me, and may I receive grace freely. *Amen.*

Luke 14:15-24

¹⁵One of the dinner guests, on hearing this, said to him, "Blessed is anyone who will eat bread in the kingdom of God!" ¹⁶Then Jesus said to him, "Someone gave a great dinner and invited many. ¹⁷At the time for the dinner he sent his slave to say to those who had been invited, 'Come; for everything is ready now.' ¹⁸But they all alike began to make excuses. The first said to him, 'I have bought a piece of land, and I must go out and see it; please accept my regrets.' ¹⁹Another said, 'I have bought five yoke of oxen, and I am going to try them out; please accept my regrets.' ²⁰Another said, 'I have just been married, and therefore I cannot come.' ²¹So the slave returned and reported this to his master. Then the owner of the house became angry and said to his slave, 'Go out at once into the streets and lanes of the town and bring in the poor, the crippled, the blind, and the lame.' ²²And the slave said, 'Sir, what you ordered has been done, and there is still room." ²³Then the master said to the slave, 'Go out into the roads and lanes, and compel people to come in, so that my house may be filled. ²⁴For I tell you, none of those who were invited will taste my dinner.'"

Reflection

This is the good news—and a new approach. Our Lord Jesus Christ invites us to a deeper understanding about the kingdom of God by offering us a banquet image of a party of joy and harmony where all are invited and included. For us, this image is a powerful parallel to the ministry of music. What is a feast—a banquet or a celebration—without music?

That kind of party is impossible.

From the beginning of the universe, there has been an open invitation to the Banquet of Music—music that plays in the soul of each of us, expressed in instruments or voices. And God sees that this is good.

But we turned against God when we limited ourselves and refused to include everyone in the Banquet of Music. We even used some types of our music to exclude certain people. As God's creation, the invitation to the Banquet of Music is to be offered to all.

This passage from Luke inspires our ministry in music as we continue to work for a better world. In this passage and in music, everyone gathers, works, shares, and helps each other, regardless of gender and socio-economic background. This means there is, and always will be, a place for everyone in the kingdom of God.

Putting together people from different social strata is a huge challenge for us in our music school. But when we give the children instruments or ask them to use their voices to play together, the result is amazing, extraordinary, and valuable. They don't understand what they are doing until they begin the first note, until they feel the necessity to look at each other for a perfect sound. They learn the magic of playing and singing together, of living together, sharing, and helping each other.

The Rev. G. David Cesar
Ecole de Musique Sainte Trinite
Port-au-Prince, Haiti

The Rev. Stephen Davenport
Episcopal Diocese of Washington
Washington, D.C.

Questions

What activities or groups exist in your community that might help you to get together with others?

How have you ever experienced the beauty of music in your life? What feelings come to your mind when you recall these moments?

Have you ever experienced exclusion in your life?

Prayer

By the power of your Holy Spirit, bring to us, O God, the joy to work together for a better world. May we speak with one voice against exclusion, injustice, and fear. Comfort all people who have been victims of violence and anger. Unite all people in music to bring people together for love, peace, and freedom in the world. Through Jesus Christ our Lord, who lives and reigns with you and the Holy Spirit, one God for ever and ever. *Amen.*

Luke 19:1-10

19 He entered Jericho and was passing through it. ²A man was there named Zacchaeus; he was a chief tax collector and was rich. ³He was trying to see who Jesus was, but on account of the crowd he could not, because he was short in stature. ⁴So he ran ahead and climbed a sycamore tree to see him, because he was going to pass that way. ⁵When Jesus came to the place, he looked up and said to him, "Zacchaeus, hurry and come down; for I must stay at your house today." ⁶So he hurried down and was happy to welcome him. ⁷All who saw it began to grumble and said, "He has gone to be the guest of one who is a sinner." ⁸Zacchaeus stood there and said to the Lord, "Look, half of my possessions, Lord, I will give to the poor; and if I have defrauded anyone of anything, I will pay back four times as much." ⁹Then Jesus said to him, "Today salvation has come to this house, because he too is a son of Abraham. ¹⁰For the Son of Man came to seek out and to save the lost."

Reflection

It's amazing how Jesus enters into our lives—coming and seeking us out. Whether we're the smallest, the most undeserving, the least likely, the hated, or the haughty, Jesus comes to save us. In Jesus' mind, we are all children of God and worthy of salvation. But in having many gifts, we are also a people of choice.

All too often, we choose to maintain our comfortable station in life. We choose greed over generosity, selfishness over sacrifice, and ambition over righteousness.

Zacchaeus is a tax collector, socially enslaved by the Roman government. Caught up in the injustice of corrupt government control, he doubles the sin, abusing the system, stealing from the citizens to assure his own wealth. A sinner's life is wearing on Zacchaeus. He is lonely and lost, craving a call to correction. The crowd has no use for this small man, riddled with corruption. But Jesus, our Lord, the Son of Man, comes to seek all of us out and to save each one.

My young friend Isaac came seeking salvation for his family and found it in education. Isaac, barely a teenager, became the sole caregiver for his siblings after South Sudanese rebel forces murdered his parents. Often, he would climb into the low hanging trees to keep watch, hoping the soldiers wouldn't come and recruit him to fight. Through the beating of the drums, Isaac heard the good news of Hope and Resurrection Secondary School opening in Atiabe, South Sudan.

Knowing that sound education can be a saving grace, Isaac walked ten miles from his home to the school gates and asked to be admitted. Two years ago, Isaac graduated and now teaches peace and reconciliation in his community. Through Christ and a solid education, Isaac lives a changed life—a saved life—a life of hope and promise for a future away from war and hatred.

The Rev. Hillary T. West
Epiphany Episcopal Church
Oak Hill, Virginia

Questions

Where have you found yourself fearful because of a corrupt system?

What actions are you called to take in the educational system, in this country or in others, to bring about change and reconciliation?

Prayer

Redeeming, saving Lord, you know our ways. You seek and save. Come now, Lord God, into our hearts and minds and souls with your saving love. Bring us hope. Show us possibility. Change our ways that we may be agents of mercy, hope, and resurrection. *Amen.*

John 1:1-16

1 In the beginning was the Word, and the Word was with God, and the Word was God. ²He was in the beginning with God. ³All things came into being through him, and without him not one thing came into being. What has come into being ⁴in him was life, and the life was the light of all people. ⁵The light shines in the darkness, and the darkness did not overcome it.

⁶There was a man sent from God, whose name was John. ⁷He came as a witness to testify to the light, so that all might believe through him. ⁸He himself was not the light, but he came to testify to the light. ⁹The true light, which enlightens everyone, was coming into the world.

¹⁰He was in the world, and the world came into being through him; yet the world did not know him. ¹¹He came to what was his own, and his own people did not accept him. ¹²But to all who received him, who believed in his name, he gave power to become children of God, ¹³who were born, not of blood or of the will of the flesh or of the will of man, but of God.

¹⁴And the Word became flesh and lived among us, and we have seen his glory, the glory as of a father's only son, full of grace and truth. ¹⁵(John testified to him and cried out, "This was he of whom I said, 'He who comes after me ranks ahead of me because he was before me.'") ¹⁶From his fullness we have all received, grace upon grace.

Reflection

The opening chapter of John's Gospel proclaims that the Word who became flesh and lived among us is the agent of creation. "All things came into being through him, and without him not one thing came into being." This means that all creation, including our finite humanity, is revelatory of Christ through whom it has come into being. That Christ is the agent of creation is affirmed in 1 Corinthians 8:6; Colossians 1:15-17; Hebrews 1:2,10; and also the Nicene Creed: "We believe in one Lord, Jesus Christ….Through him all things were made."

Such moments as sunrise viewed from a mountain top, a sunset across a lake, a flower, a tree, the smile of a passerby, the nuzzling of a dog can be experiences of revelation and encounter with the ever-creative Word "through whom all things were made."

All experiences of transcendence and awe in the face of life's mystery or of being overcome by the wonder of creation are points of meeting with the Word hidden within what has engaged us and drawn our attention. It can be an object, a vista, another person. "In him was life and the life was the light of all people."

"He was in the world, and the world came into being through him; yet the world did not know him." Acknowledged or not, Christ is the life-source of all living things. As such, Christ transcends the boundaries we set, such as nationality, race, religion. Through the action of the Holy Spirit, Christ continues to enliven the world and draw us beyond the limits of our understanding and imagination into the force field of God's own desire for the thriving and well-being of this planet we call home.

Bishop Frank T. Griswold
XXV Presiding Bishop of the Episcopal Church
Philadelphia, Pennsylvania

Questions

What are some of the ways in which I have experienced Christ, the Word, in creation in my own life and in the life of someone else?

How have I been changed or my perceptions of myself or others been deepened by such encounters?

Prayer

Lord Jesus Christ, Eternal Word, through whom all things have come to be: Open the eyes of my heart to see you in all things, including my own humanity. Help me to embrace the world in the power of your reconciling love, and make me a sign of that love to all. *Amen*.

John 12: 1–8

12 Six days before the Passover Jesus came to Bethany, the home of Lazarus, whom he had raised from the dead. [2]There they gave a dinner for him. Martha served, and Lazarus was one of those at the table with him. [3]Mary took a pound of costly perfume made of pure nard, anointed Jesus' feet, and wiped them with her hair. The house was filled with the fragrance of the perfume. [4]But Judas Iscariot, one of his disciples (the one who was about to betray him), said, [5]"Why was this perfume not sold for three hundred denarii and the money given to the poor?" [6](He said this not because he cared about the poor, but because he was a thief; he kept the common purse and used to steal what was put into it.) [7]Jesus said, "Leave her alone. She bought it so that she might keep it for the day of my burial. [8]You always have the poor with you, but you do not always have me."

Reflection

The power and possibilities of money dominate our lives. From government spending to charitable giving and household budgets, we regularly gravitate to the bottom line. Human hubris fuels this habit. Our models of scarcity undervalue moral, civic and spiritual considerations. We often find ourselves asking, "But what will it cost me?" or perhaps even "Why was this perfume not sold for three hundred denarii and the money given to the poor?"

At supper with the great and the good, Mary of Bethany places our obsession with money front and center at Jesus' feet. There, she gives away a most valuable possession—a pound of pure nard—for Jesus' personal honor and glory. Mary's offering is an expression of love that proclaims Jesus as Lord and Savior. He is rightly the center of being, and only through God's Messiah will the world be ultimately healed. Everyone in that dining room was dumbfounded, and many of us too.

For over twenty-five years, I have encountered the power and the possibilities of people offering their highest hopes and their best efforts in Jerusalem, Israel, and Palestine. Every day, Jewish, Christian, and Muslim civilian peace-builders—often against great odds and always at great personal cost—dedicate themselves to the transformation of two peoples plagued by violence, bigotry, poverty and oppression for centuries.

Each year, the peoples living in the Holy Land receive more financial and military aid than all other groups of people on this Earth. And yet the poor remain with us and peace eludes us. The failure of weaponry, construction loans, and high-tech to deliver freedom or convert the human heart rightly questions our money-centered approach. It is here that we encounter our friend Mary.

Transforming the cultural violence that undergirds both Israeli and Palestinian society requires deliberately helping ordinary children, women, and men to experience one another as human beings with the same needs, hopes, and fears. This is a slow, non-linear process, involving frustration, progress, and the difficult acceptance that the hardness of our human hearts—the primary source of our suffering—can and will only be healed by God's grace.

The Rev. Nicholas T. Porter
Jerusalem Peacebuilders, Inc.
Battleboro, Vermont

Questions

What are the expressions of cultural violence in your community?

Why do we undervalue moral, civic and spiritual goals in the face of financial ones?

What is your most valuable possession awaiting to be offered to the Lord's service?

Prayer

O Lord of Life, we remember before you the poor—all those who suffer from hunger, violence, oppression, and dispossession. Empower them with new possibilities and an abiding sense of your love. Empower us with the kindness, strength, and courage to serve them. Together, make us instruments of your peace and witnesses of your grace. All this we pray through the love and mercy of Christ Jesus, our advocate. *Amen.*

Acts 6:1-15

6 Now during those days, when the disciples were increasing in number, the Hellenists complained against the Hebrews because their widows were being neglected in the daily distribution of food. [2]And the twelve called together the whole community of the disciples and said, "It is not right that we should neglect the word of God in order to wait on tables. [3]Therefore, friends, select from among yourselves seven men of good standing, full of the Spirit and of wisdom, whom we may appoint to this task, [4]while we, for our part, will devote ourselves to prayer and to serving the word." [5]What they said pleased the whole community, and they chose Stephen, a man full of faith and the Holy Spirit, together with Philip, Prochorus, Nicanor, Timon, Parmenas, and Nicolaus, a proselyte of Antioch.

[6]They had these men stand before the apostles, who prayed and laid their hands on them.

[7]The word of God continued to spread; the number of the disciples increased greatly in Jerusalem, and a great many of the priests became obedient to the faith.

[8]Stephen, full of grace and power, did great wonders and signs among the people. [9]Then some of those who belonged to the synagogue of the Freedmen (as it was called), Cyrenians, Alexandrians, and others of those from Cilicia and Asia, stood up and argued with Stephen.

[10]But they could not withstand the wisdom and the Spirit with which he spoke. [11]Then they secretly instigated some men to say, "We have heard him speak blasphemous words against Moses and God." [12]They stirred

up the people as well as the elders and the scribes; then they suddenly confronted him, seized him, and brought him before the council. ¹³They set up false witnesses who said, "This man never stops saying things against this holy place and the law; ¹⁴for we have heard him say that this Jesus of Nazareth will destroy this place and will change the customs that Moses handed on to us." ¹⁵And all who sat in the council looked intently at him, and they saw that his face was like the face of an angel.

Reflection

Reading the story of Acts 6:1-6 about the Hellenist widows reminds me of a conference I attended where widows were given special attention. On the last day of the conference, the leader called on all widows who were attending the conference to stand and receive special prayers. The women stood in a line, and the guest preacher offered a prayer. After the prayers, the leader passed around a basket with envelopes and asked each widow to pick one. The leader shared that the congregation had taken up a special collection for the widows to show them that they knew their plight and not only were they praying for the widows but they also wanted to give them a special gift.

The widows in this story from the book of Acts are not people of privilege. They speak a different language and live on the margins of the emerging Christian community. The plight of these widows and the action on their behalf is a lesson to us about how to deal with the plight of those like the widows who are voiceless, powerless, exploited, and oppressed.

First, the community carefully appoints people who speak the language of the widows, are of good repute, and are able to take care of the bereaved women. Second, the care of widows is the first social service undertaken by the community, and third, the widows are supported on the basis of their need and not their status. The widows represent those in our society who are voiceless, powerless, and exploited. All of our communities have widows. Whatever name we give to them, the test of the church is how we treat them.

Esther M. Mombo
St. Paul's University
Limuru, Kenya

Questions

Are there prejudices against widows in your society? How are they expressed? Name or describe groups in your community who are like the widows in this story from the book of Acts. In what ways should your church and your community provide physical, economic, social, and spiritual support and encouragement to widows?

In a society where a donor mentality grips all of our actions, how does the story of these widows help us support those in need without trying to maintain our own honor or status as donors?

Prayer

O God, your word tells us that true religion is to look after orphans and widows in their distress. Forgive us when we overlook the needs of the widows in our congregations and communities. Through the power of the Holy Spirit, cause us to listen to their voices and those whom they represent. Give us wisdom to hear their cries of distress and to comfort them. This we ask in Jesus' name. *Amen.*

Philemon 1-25

1 Paul, a prisoner of Christ Jesus, and Timothy our brother, To Philemon our dear friend and co-worker, 2to Apphia our sister, to Archippus our fellow soldier, and to the church in your house: 3Grace to you and peace from God our Father and the Lord Jesus Christ.

4When I remember you in my prayers, I always thank my God 5because I hear of your love for all the saints and your faith toward the Lord Jesus. 6I pray that the sharing of your faith may become effective when you perceive all the good that we may do for Christ. 7I have indeed received much joy and encouragement from your love, because the hearts of the saints have been refreshed through you, my brother.

8For this reason, though I am bold enough in Christ to command you to do your duty, 9yet I would rather appeal to you on the basis of love—and I, Paul, do this as an old man, and now also as a prisoner of Christ Jesus. 10I am appealing to you for my child, Onesimus, whose father I have become during my imprisonment. 11Formerly he was useless to you, but now he is indeed useful both to you and to me. 12I am sending him, that is, my own heart, back to you. 13I wanted to keep him with me, so that he might be of service to me in your place during my imprisonment for the gospel; 14but I preferred to do nothing without your consent, in order that your good deed might be voluntary and not something forced. 15Perhaps this is the reason he was separated from you for a while, so that you might have him back forever, 16no longer as a slave but more than a slave, a beloved brother—

especially to me but how much more to you, both in the flesh and in the Lord.

¹⁷So if you consider me your partner, welcome him as you would welcome me. ¹⁸If he has wronged you in any way, or owes you anything, charge that to my account. ¹⁹I, Paul, am writing this with my own hand: I will repay it. I say nothing about your owing me even your own self. ²⁰Yes, brother, let me have this benefit from you in the Lord! Refresh my heart in Christ.

²¹Confident of your obedience, I am writing to you, knowing that you will do even more than I say.

²²One thing more—prepare a guest room for me, for I am hoping through your prayers to be restored to you.

²³Epaphras, my fellow prisoner in Christ Jesus, sends greetings to you, ²⁴and so do Mark, Aristarchus, Demas, and Luke, my fellow workers.

²⁵The grace of the Lord Jesus Christ be with your spirit.

Reflection

The book of Philemon is a mere 25 verses, a brief letter from Paul to Philemon and his friends about a slave who has become a follower of Jesus. The slave's name is Onesimus, and he has established a relationship with Paul while Paul has been in prison. His owner is a Christian named Philemon, who owes his conversion to Paul.

We do not know how Philemon responded to the letter from Paul, nor do we know what Onesimus thought about it. In Philemon, we do not hear from Onesimus.

I have so many questions about this letter. I wonder what Onesimus wants? He is a Christian and is free in Christ. Why does Paul write as though Onesimus' freedom in this life is contingent upon being freed by his Christian owner? Why is it the owner's imperative to be free Onesimus, and not Onesimus's imperative to simply claim his freedom as a Christian?

Can you imagine asking Harriett Tubman to go back to her slave owner and turn herself in so that a Christian slave owner could behave as a Christian should? Is the slave merely a passive site of a "mission-driven" Christian action of the slave owner?

What is Paul trying to do? Scholars point out that these few verses are carefully constructed. Paul is delicately trying to create the right outcome, proving what Philemon owes to Jesus and the community of faith. I hope Philemon ended up doing the right thing, but I wonder if the carefully worded letter means that Paul does not think Philemon will be agreeable.

I like to think that Onesimus did not return to Philemon. In my mind, Paul and Philemon have it out in an interesting correspondence, but Onesimus shakes his head at them and goes off in another direction to tell the good news: that he was once a slave and only knew himself as a slave, but now he is free in Christ.

The Rev. Winnie Varghese
Trinity Church, Wall Street
New York City, New York

Questions

Can you recall a time when someone decided what was best for you without consulting you?

What does freedom in Christ mean to you?

Prayer

God, our freedom, you have made us for joy. Give us hearts of compassion to know the world in your love. Give us the courage to know our own dignity and the curiosity to seek out those whose voices we are not used to hearing. Give us your passion for justice, and open our eyes a little bit more, just a little bit more, that we may see you. *Amen.*

Hebrews 13:1-25

13 Let mutual love continue. ²Do not neglect to show hospitality to strangers, for by doing that some have entertained angels without knowing it. ³Remember those who are in prison, as though you were in prison with them; those who are being tortured, as though you yourselves were being tortured. ⁴Let marriage be held in honor by all, and let the marriage bed be kept undefiled; for God will judge fornicators and adulterers. ⁵Keep your lives free from the love of money, and be content with what you have; for he has said, "I will never leave you or forsake you." ⁶So we can say with confidence, "The Lord is my helper; I will not be afraid. What can anyone do to me?"

⁷Remember your leaders, those who spoke the word of God to you; consider the outcome of their way of life, and imitate their faith. ⁸Jesus Christ is the same yesterday and today and forever. ⁹Do not be carried away by all kinds of strange teachings; for it is well for the heart to be strengthened by grace, not by regulations about food, which have not benefited those who observe them. ¹⁰We have an altar from which those who officiate in the tent have no right to eat. ¹¹For the bodies of those animals whose blood is brought into the sanctuary by the high priest as a sacrifice for sin are burned outside the camp. ¹²Therefore Jesus also suffered outside the city gate in order to sanctify the people by his own blood. ¹³Let us then go to him outside the camp and bear the abuse he endured. ¹⁴For here we have no lasting city, but we are looking for the city that is to come. ¹⁵Through him, then, let us continually offer a sacrifice of praise to God, that

is, the fruit of lips that confess his name. [16]Do not neglect to do good and to share what you have, for such sacrifices are pleasing to God.

[17]Obey your leaders and submit to them, for they are keeping watch over your souls and will give an account. Let them do this with joy and not with sighing—for that would be harmful to you.

[18]Pray for us; we are sure that we have a clear conscience, desiring to act honorably in all things. [19]I urge you all the more to do this, so that I may be restored to you very soon.

[20]Now may the God of peace, who brought back from the dead our Lord Jesus, the great shepherd of the sheep, by the blood of the eternal covenant, [21]make you complete in everything good so that you may do his will, working among us that which is pleasing in his sight, through Jesus Christ, to whom be the glory forever and ever. Amen.

[22]I appeal to you, brothers and sisters, bear with my word of exhortation, for I have written to you briefly. [23]I want you to know that our brother Timothy has been set free; and if he comes in time, he will be with me when I see you. [24]Greet all your leaders and all the saints. Those from Italy send you greetings. [25]Grace be with all of you.

Reflection

Some 5 million children, or roughly 7 percent of all children living in the U.S., have a parent currently or previously incarcerated. Between 33 million and 36.5 million children—nearly half the total population of American children—have at least one parent with a criminal record.

Located in North Philadelphia, St. James Episcopal Middle School enrolls sixty-four students. All are living at or below the poverty line, many living in deep poverty, and nearly all have at least one relative currently in prison. On the east side of our neighborhood, one of the drug stores has a large billboard advertisement that reads "We ship to prisons." Each morning during prayer, students pray "please" and "thank you" prayers. Students often pray for relatives who are "away." Incarceration is an all too familiar reality for our students and their families.

We recently learned that Tymir's father was "away" until 2026—serving time at a high security federal prison in Western Pennsylvania. Tymir was making great progress at our school. We knew that nothing would motivate Tymir more than knowing that his dad was aware of his progress.

A teacher decided to learn more about Tymir's father's status and was able to find the name and location of the prison. After several months of communication with prison employees, contact was made with the prison chaplain. After maneuvering through a series of security clearances, our school was granted permission to connect, in writing, with Tymir's father. With much excitement, we began to forward regular updates to him, including Tymir's desire to attend one of the best high schools in the region.

During this time, Tymir's father became increasingly involved with writing for the *Freebird*, the prison's internal monthly newsletter written and published by inmates. Tymir's father often wrote about his son's positive trajectory and promise. Because of his positive involvement with *Freebird*, Tymir's father was granted permission for his son to visit.

Our school's spring break fell several weeks after this exciting development. With no transportation available to the prison's rural location, Tymir had no way to visit his father. Two teachers eagerly stepped forward to drive Tymir to visit his father, sacrificing their well-deserved spring break.

This scripture from Hebrews invokes various ways we are to practice loving each other and offering brotherly and sisterly charity with those on the fringes of society. And if we can do these kind things, and if we can start to do them a little more, then we might find that our hearts turn more and more to God.

We may not know anyone in jail, but 33 million children in our country know someone. Let us remember our brothers and sisters who are in prison, and remember that they and their children need our kindness and love.

David Kasievich
St. James Episcopal School
Philadelphia, Pennsylvania

Questions

How can faith communities move young people from incarceration to education?

If corruption and abuse are being carried out in our names inside our prisons—the prisons we pay for—how can we, as citizens in a democracy, take responsibility for what is going on and change it? To what action do you, personally, feel drawn? (Examples: talk with your state house or state assembly representative or senator, raise the issue at your church, start conversations in your community, etc.)

Prayer

God, we pray for your love and mercy for those who are in prison that your love might reach them through our efforts. We can't imagine the dark, sorrowful, desperate paths that have led up to this period of life for those in prison. We pray for the family members of those in prison, especially their sons and daughters. Encourage and strengthen them. Provide for their needs. Hear their prayers and comfort them daily.

We know that the road to recovery for our brothers and sisters in prison will not be an easy one. Help them to find those who truly love them with the love of the Lord; people who will be mentors, friends and prayer partners on their journey of healing and wholeness. We pray especially for prison chaplains, teachers, social workers, caring family members, and fellow inmates who comfort those who are incarcerated. We rejoice in your mercy and exalt and praise Your Holy Name: Father, Son and Holy Spirit, both now and ever and unto the ages of ages. *Amen.*

James 1:19—2:17

[19]You must understand this, my beloved: let everyone be quick to listen, slow to speak, slow to anger; [20]for your anger does not produce God's righteousness. [21]Therefore rid yourselves of all sordidness and rank growth of wickedness, and welcome with meekness the implanted word that has the power to save your souls.

[22]But be doers of the word, and not merely hearers who deceive themselves. [23]For if any are hearers of the word and not doers, they are like those who look at themselves in a mirror; [24]for they look at themselves and, on going away, immediately forget what they were like. [25]But those who look into the perfect law, the law of liberty, and persevere, being not hearers who forget but doers who act—they will be blessed in their doing.

[26]If any think they are religious, and do not bridle their tongues but deceive their hearts, their religion is worthless. [27]Religion that is pure and undefiled before God, the Father, is this: to care for orphans and widows in their distress, and to keep oneself unstained by the world.

2 My brothers and sisters, do you with your acts of favoritism really believe in our glorious Lord Jesus Christ? [2]For if a person with gold rings and in fine clothes comes into your assembly, and if a poor person in dirty clothes also comes in, [3]and if you take notice of the one wearing the fine clothes and say, "Have a seat here, please," while to the one who is poor you say, "Stand there," or, "Sit at my feet," [4]have you not made distinctions among yourselves, and become judges with evil thoughts?

⁵Listen, my beloved brothers and sisters. Has not God chosen the poor in the world to be rich in faith and to be heirs of the kingdom that he has promised to those who love him? ⁶But you have dishonored the poor. Is it not the rich who oppress you? Is it not they who drag you into court? ⁷Is it not they who blaspheme the excellent name that was invoked over you?

⁸You do well if you really fulfill the royal law according to the scripture, "You shall love your neighbor as yourself." ⁹But if you show partiality, you commit sin and are convicted by the law as transgressors. ¹⁰For whoever keeps the whole law but fails in one point has become accountable for all of it. ¹¹For the one who said, "You shall not commit adultery," also said, "You shall not murder." Now if you do not commit adultery but if you murder, you have become a transgressor of the law. ¹²So speak and so act as those who are to be judged by the law of liberty. ¹³For judgment will be without mercy to anyone who has shown no mercy; mercy triumphs over judgment.

¹⁴What good is it, my brothers and sisters, if you say you have faith but do not have works? Can faith save you? ¹⁵If a brother or sister is naked and lacks daily food, ¹⁶and one of you says to them, "Go in peace; keep warm and eat your fill," and yet you do not supply their bodily needs, what is the good of that? ¹⁷So faith by itself, if it has no works, is dead.

Reflection

The Epistle of James is attributed to the brother of our Lord. James was a leader among the first Christians in Jerusalem. As the fourteenth Anglican Bishop in Jerusalem and the Anglican Archbishop in Jerusalem, it is my privilege to testify to this teaching and healing still present in the Holy Land today.

The Diocese of Jerusalem is diverse, encompassing faith communities from five countries—Lebanon, Syria, Jordan, Palestine, and Israel. It ministers in some of the most difficult situations, aware that Christians are finding it ever harder to exist in communities in the Middle East. The diocese provides solace, comfort, and livelihoods to refugees from Syria and Iraq. It reaches out, as Saint James urges all Christians, "to care for orphans and widows in their distress." This diocese's provision of healthcare with hospitals in Gaza and Nablus and rehabilitation centers in Jerusalem, Beirut, and Jordan are responses to this call. This may be seen as the *missio dei* of this diocese: a prayerful presence serving the poorest and most marginalized in the community.

This work is not founded in secular philanthropy but rather a deep faith that the gospel is alive in our work and is a proclamation that Christ is for all. Jesus Christ died to save us from ourselves, our sins, our selfishness, and our egos. He rose again to give us confidence to walk his path in love—a love that casts out fear and urges us to seek the liberty that he promises: God's kingdom on earth as it is in heaven.

The liberty that Christ promises to our souls requires us to work for the liberty and dignity of each and every community in which we minister. The prayer of this diocese is rooted in the desire for the peace of Jerusalem—physically, spiritually, and universally. It is not only our prayer; it is our action too. In the Holy Land, we seek to say less and do more with our prayers and service: "But those who look into the perfect law, the law of liberty, and persevere, being not hearers who forget but doers who act—they will be blessed in their doing."

Archbishop Suheil Dawani
Diocese of Jerusalem
Jerusalem, Israel

Questions _____

Saint James' letter is sometimes criticized for placing more emphasis on works than faith. How do we see our work day-by-day reflected in our faith? How can we make our faith more relevant and real in our work?

Saint James begins this passage with an admonition that we should rid ourselves of all wickedness and welcome with meekness the implanted word that has the power to save souls. We are called to be humble before God, for our hearts to be open to his word. Can you still yourselves to allow that word to be implanted in your hearts and your souls?

Saint James calls for practical action—to reach out to the marginalized. Who are the marginalized you encounter—the poor person on the street, the lonely neighbor—whose hearts can be touched by your kindness today?

On Maundy Thursday, it has become the tradition that the Anglican Archbishop is invited to read the gospel at the Armenian Cathedral of Saing James. The Armenian Patriarch sits down and with a bowl of water washes each of his bishops' feet before blessing them with butter (Armenia does not have olive trees, so butter is traditionally used), symbolizing how our Lord washed his disciple's feet. Whose feet need washing? Whose feet need care? Who needs love?

In the Holy Land the indigenous Christians are called the Living Stones (Luke 19:40). The Living Stones minister in this place not just for their own benefit but on behalf of all Christians for all. How can you be Living Stones where you live?

Prayer

Lord, giver of all good things in this world: Grant to your servants your light in their hearts to kindle deep within a faith inspired through your Word, revealing that in tenderness and compassion, all may be allowed to live in liberty and with dignity; and may the peace of Jerusalem be cradled as a reality for all your creation. We ask this humbly through your Son, our Savior, Jesus Christ. *Amen.*

1 John 4:1-21

4 Beloved, do not believe every spirit, but test the spirits to see whether they are from God; for many false prophets have gone out into the world. ²By this you know the Spirit of God: every spirit that confesses that Jesus Christ has come in the flesh is from God, ³and every spirit that does not confess Jesus is not from God. And this is the spirit of the antichrist, of which you have heard that it is coming; and now it is already in the world. ⁴Little children, you are from God, and have conquered them; for the one who is in you is greater than the one who is in the world. ⁵They are from the world; therefore what they say is from the world, and the world listens to them. ⁶We are from God. Whoever knows God listens to us, and whoever is not from God does not listen to us. From this we know the spirit of truth and the spirit of error.

⁷Beloved, let us love one another, because love is from God; everyone who loves is born of God and knows God. ⁸Whoever does not love does not know God, for God is love. ⁹God's love was revealed among us in this way: God sent his only Son into the world so that we might live through him. ¹⁰In this is love, not that we loved God but that he loved us and sent his Son to be the atoning sacrifice for our sins. ¹¹Beloved, since God loved us so much, we also ought to love one another. ¹²No one has ever seen God; if we love one another, God lives in us, and his love is perfected in us.

¹³By this we know that we abide in him and he in us, because he has given us of his Spirit. ¹⁴And

we have seen and do testify that the Father has sent his Son as the Savior of the world. [15]God abides in those who confess that Jesus is the Son of God, and they abide in God. [16]So we have known and believe the love that God has for us.

God is love, and those who abide in love abide in God, and God abides in them. [17]Love has been perfected among us in this: that we may have boldness on the day of judgment, because as he is, so are we in this world. [18]There is no fear in love, but perfect love casts out fear; for fear has to do with punishment, and whoever fears has not reached perfection in love. [19]We love because he first loved us. [20]Those who say, "I love God," and hate their brothers or sisters, are liars; for those who do not love a brother or sister whom they have seen, cannot love God whom they have not seen. [21]The commandment we have from him is this: those who love God must love their brothers and sisters also.

Reflection

God is love. We know that, don't we? Do we need to define love, or can we assume that love is thinking about the other and how our behavior affects others? It has always been important to me to know how others interpret my actions and what effect my behavior has on them. Loving God plays out in love for our brothers and sisters. If we do it right, our love for God is demonstrated by our treatment of each other and how our behavior impacts our neighbors.

Behavior matters. It matters to our neighbors, and it matters to God. It is precisely this concern that drew me into my ministry, which is a religious response to global warming. If we love our brothers and sisters, we wouldn't pollute their air, water or land. God says to love one another. How can we be silent and still when what God loves—all of creation—is being destroyed?

We are destroying the garden that we were put here to till and to keep. Global warming is destroying creation, species, and habitats, and thousands of communities are suffering from heat, drought, fires, and collapsing coastlines. It is a well-documented fact that poor communities and countries around the world suffer the most from human-induced climate change. These are the same communities God is calling us to serve.

The time is now to do all in our power to stop the warming trend that adversely affects the least among us, those who have contributed little to the problem and have the least ability to adapt to sea rise, crop disruption, and severe weather events. We can show our love for God, for each other, and for our neighbors by cutting our fossil fuel consumption and electing legislators who understand the science behind climate change. This is a social justice issue and a moral responsibility. We need to recognize that poverty and climate are directly connected.

The Rev. Canon Sally Bingham
The Regeneration Project:
Interfaith Power and Light Campaign
San Francisco, California

Questions _____

How might you show your neighbors that you love them?

What can you do to decrease carbon emissions?

Prayer _____

Gracious God, open our hearts to the realization that we have not been good stewards of your creation. Give us the courage and inspiration to do better. Help us to lead others and show our love for you in how we treat what you love, the creation and all our brothers and sisters. *Amen.*

Additional Biblical Texts
Focusing on Social Justice

OLD TESTAMENT LESSONS

Genesis 41:1:36, 53-57—Joseph interpreting the king's dream about the famine and providing for the needy

Genesis 45:1-20—Joseph provides for his brothers even though they sold him into slavery

Exodus 1:1-22—The Israelites live as slaves in Egypt and have their male children slaughtered

Exodus 18:1-27—God helps Moses create a judicial system to hear people's complaints

Exodus 20:1-20—God gives Moses the Ten Commandments

Exodus 21:1-36—The just treatment of slaves and other ethical considerations

Exodus 22:1-31—Property laws and laws for community life

Leviticus 5:1-11—A sliding scale of sin offerings to accommodate the poor

Leviticus 6:1-7; 12:1-8; 14:21-23—Accommodations are made to help the poor observe laws of purity

Leviticus 25:1-28—Honoring the sabbatical/Jubilee Year

Leviticus 25:35-55—God's commands for caring for the poor and needy

Deuteronomy 1:9-18—Impartial justice for citizens and foreigners alike, rich and poor

Deuteronomy 5:1-22—God gave the Ten Commandments to ensure justice and care for all

Deuteronomy 15:1-18—On forgiving loans and freeing slaves

Deuteronomy 16:9-15; 17:8-13; 18-20—Inclusion of the poor, widows, foreigners, and orphans in festivals and observances

Deuteronomy 24:10-22; 25:13-14—Don't withhold pay and treat orphans and foreigners well and fairly

Joshua 20:1-9—Creation of cities of refuge for persons who have accidentally killed someone

Ruth 2:1-23—Boaz provides for Ruth the foreigner so that she and Naomi might survive

1 Chronicles 16:7-22—God is bringing justice everywhere on earth

2 Chronicles 19:4-11—Judges must never be bribed and all crimes must be adjudicated

Nehemiah 5:1-19—Nehemiah's concern for the poor

Job 24:1-25—Why doesn't God take better care of the poor

Job 27:13-23—God will turn the tables on the rich who neglect the poor

Job 29:12-17; 31:1-28, 38-40—Job maintains his case as a model of human justice

Psalm 37:1-40—The LORD loves justice, and he won't ever desert his faithful people

Psalm 68:1-35—Our God, from your sacred home you take care of orphans and protect widows

Psalm 69:1-36—The LORD will listen when the homeless cry out… and his people in prison

Psalm 82:1-8—Be fair to the poor and to orphans. Defend the helpless and everyone in need

Psalm 85:1-13—Justice will march in front, making a path for you to follow

Psalm 94:1-23—Justice and fairness will go hand in hand, and all who do right will follow along.

Psalm 101:1-8—I refuse to be corrupt or to take part in anything crooked

Psalm 146:1-10—The LORD sets prisoners free and heals the blind eyes.

Proverbs 11:1-31—The LORD hates anyone who cheats, but he likes everyone who is honest

Proverbs 19:1-20—Caring for the poor is lending to the LORD, and you will be well repaid.

Proverbs 22:1-16—The LORD blesses everyone who gives food to the poor

Proverbs 28:1-28—Criminals do not know what justice means

Proverbs 29:1-27—Without guidance from God, law and order disappear

Proverbs 31:8-29—You must defend those who are helpless

Ecclesiastes 5:8-9—The poor are abused because lower officials must do what higher ups order

Isaiah 1:12-17—Stop doing wrong and learn to live right, defend widows and orphans

Isaiah 2:1-22—They will pound their swords and their spears, they will never make war

Isaiah 3:10-15—You have crushed my people and rubbed in the dirt the faces of the poor

Isaiah 10:1-2—You have made cruel and unfair laws and rob widows and orphans

Isaiah 11:1-9—But with righteousness shall he judge the poor

Isaiah 29:15-21—The deaf will be able to hear whatever is read to them, the blind will be freed

Isaiah 32:15-20—When the Spirit is given to us from heaven… justice will produce lasting peace

Jeremiah 22:1-3, 13-19—You have been allowing people to cheat, rob and take advantage; exhortation to repent

Lamentations 2:11-15—My people are being wiped out, and children lie helpless

Lamentations 3:22-40—Don't trample the prisoners under your feet or cheat anyone

Zechariah 7:4-13—Do not oppress the widow, the fatherless, the sojourner, or the poor

NEW TESTAMENT LESSONS

Matthew 5:1-32—The Sermon on the Mount and dealing with anger and divorce

Matthew 5:38-48—Jesus' teaching about love and revenge and turning the other cheek

Matthew 6:1-4—Jesus' admonition not to flaunt what you have done to aid the poor

Matthew 9:9-13—Jesus chooses Matthew, a despised tax collector, to follow him

Matthew 18:21-34—Jesus tells a story about a person who refuses to forgive

Mark 11:15-19—Jesus overturns the tables of the money changers in the Temple

Mark 12:38-44—Jesus condemns the Pharisees and teachers while applauding the widow's mite

Mark 14:3-9—The story of the woman anointing Jesus' feet with expensive perfume

Luke 3:1-20—John the Baptist urges his listeners to be generous and honest with all

Luke 6:20-49—God will bless the poor and his kingdom belongs to those who are poor

Luke 12:13-34—The Parable of the Rich Fool who stored up for a future he did not have

Luke 16:19-31—Jesus tells the Parable of Lazarus and the Rich Man

Luke 18:1-8—Parable of the Widow and the Unjust Judge

Acts 2:14-47—Give the money to whoever needs it

Acts 4:32-37—They would give the money to whoever needed it

Romans 12:1-21—Take care of God's needy people and welcome strangers into your home

Romans 15:14-32—Delivering money for God's needy people

2 Corinthians 8:1-15—Encouraging generosity

Galatians 2:1-10—Remember the poor

Philippians 4:10-23—I know what it is to be poor or to have plenty…It was good of you to help me

1 Timothy 5:1-6—A warning about material possessions

James 5:1-20—The Lord All-Powerful has surely heard the cries of the workers

Revelation 21:1-8—God will wipe all tears from their eyes, and there will be no more death…

PROVERBS

Proverbs 2:1-9 (or 8-9)—God sees that justice is done and watches over everyone

Proverbs 3:32-33 (or 32-35)—God does not like people who are dishonest

Proverbs 6:16-19—God doesn't like people who tell lies or murder

Proverbs 6:29-35—The punishment for adultery and theft

Proverbs 8:12-16—If you respect God, you will hate what is evil

Proverbs 10:1-5—Laziness leads to poverty, hard work leads to wealth

Proverbs 10:15-16—If you live right, your reward will be a good life

Proverbs 10:27—If you live a just life, your life will be lengthened

Proverbs 11:1-7—The Lord detests those who cheat

Proverbs 11:9-19—A city with bad leaders will be destroyed: do the right thing and be rewarded

Proverbs 11:24-28—Generosity will be rewarded; strive always to do the right thing

Proverbs 11:29-31—Those who are cruel and mean will be punished

Proverbs 13:5-6—Live right and you will be safe

Proverbs 13:11—Money earned unjustly will disappear

Proverbs 13:23-25—Even when the poor have a good harvest, they get cheated

Proverbs 14:1-5—An honest person always tells the truth; a dishonest person tells lies

Proverbs 14:20-25—Hard work leads to wealth; empty talk leads to poverty

Proverbs 14:31—If you mistreat the poor, you insult God

Proverbs 15:15-16—It is better to obey the Lord and be poor than to be rich and confused

Proverbs 15:25-27—You protect yourself by refusing bribes

Proverbs 16:8—It is better to be honest and poor than dishonest and rich

Proverbs 16:11-12—Leaders should hate evil and love honesty and truth

Proverbs 16:16-19—You are better off being humble and poor than rich and stripped of wealth

Proverbs 17:5—You will be punished if you make fun of someone in trouble

Proverbs 17:15—God does not like those who defend the guilty

Proverbs 18:5—It is wrong to deny the innocent from getting justice

Proverbs 19:1-10—Dishonest witnesses and liars won't escape punishment

Proverbs 19:15-17—Caring for the poor is like lending to the Lord

Proverbs 19:22—Honesty matters most; it is better to be poor than to be a liar

Proverbs 20:10-13—God detests those who use dishonest scales and measures

Proverbs 20:21-23—Getting rich quickly may be a curse; wait upon the Lord to help you

Proverbs 20:26—A wise ruler severely punishes every criminal

Proverbs 21:1:6—Cheating to get rich is a foolish dream

Proverbs 21:28-29—God's people are reliable in the courts of justice

Proverbs 22:1-16—The Lord blesses everyone who gives food to the poor

Proverbs 22:22-23—Don't take advantage of the poor in court

Proverbs 23:10—Don't swindle others from their land because God will defend the harmed

Proverbs 24:24-29—Punish the guilty, but never accuse someone who is not guilty

Proverbs 25:5—Evil people must be removed before a leader can lead with justice

Proverbs 25:21-22—Give your enemies something to eat and drink, and God will reward you

Proverbs 28:1-28—Criminals do not know what justice means

Proverbs 29:1-27—Without guidance from God, law and order disappear

Proverbs 30:7-9—Make me absolutely honest, and give me just what I need and no more

Proverbs 31:5—Drinking makes you forget your responsibilities to care for the poor

Proverbs 31:8-9—You must defend those who are helpful and have no hope

Proverbs 31:10-29—A good wife is hard to find; she helps the poor and the needy

About the Authors

The Rev. Canon Sally Bingham was one of the first faith leaders to fully recognize global warming as a core moral issue. She has mobilized thousands to put their faith into action through energy stewardship. A recipient of the Audubon Society's Rachel Carson award, a Purpose Prize, the Energy Globe Award, and the EPA Climate Protection Award, as well as the lead author of *Love God, Heal Earth*, Sally is the founder and president of The Regeneration Project: Interfaith Power and Light Campaign, whose mission is deepening the connection between ecology and faith.

The Regeneration Project has reached more than 18,000 people through programs in forty states. Congregations of all faiths are making commitments to cut their carbon emissions and to encourage their parishioners to do the same in their homes. To learn more, visit: www.interfaithpowerandlight.org

Charles (Buck) Blanchard is the director of mission and outreach for the Diocese of Virginia. His role is to encourage and facilitate the mission and outreach efforts of all congregations in the diocese. From 1980 to 1982, Buck served in the Peace Corps in Togo, West Africa. After graduating from Washington and Lee School of Law, Buck worked as a lawyer for Hunton & Williams. He later lived in Brussels, Belgium, and helped establish the firm's European business practice and its office in Warsaw, Poland. After returning to the United States, Buck worked in the venture capital industry and ran his own private equity firm. He joined the diocesan staff in 2006.

Buck is married to the Rev. Weezie Blanchard, and they have four children. He is a strong supporter of The Peter Paul Development Center, Richmond, Virginia, which serves the children, families, and senior citizens of Richmond East End. To learn more, visit: www.peterpauldevcenter.org

Noah F. Bullock is the executive director of Cristosal, a non-profit organization based in El Salvador working to advance human rights in Central America. Cristosal is a leader in advocating for the rights of those displaced by violence, ranging from direct humanitarian and legal assistance to advocacy on a global level. Programs also include community development, participatory research, and international exchange, including opportunities to travel and study with Cristosal in El Salvador. To learn more, visit: www.cristosal.org

The Rev. Canon Jamie Callaway is the general secretary of Colleges and Universities of the Anglican Communion (CUAC). CUAC is a worldwide network that supports the mutual flourishing of its members through engaging with each other, their society, and their churches, as they seek to enable their students and faculties to become active and responsive citizens in God's world. In the Episcopal Church, these schools include Bard in Annandale-on Hudson and Hobart and William Smith Colleges in Geneva, New York; St. Augustine, a Hispanic college in Chicago; two historically black colleges and universities: St. Augustine's in Raleigh, North Carolina, and Voorhees in Denmark, South Carolina; Kenyon in Gambier, Ohio; the University of the South, Sewanee, Tennessee; Université Episcopale du Haiti in Port-au-Prince; Trinity University of Asia, Manila, Philippines; and Cuttington University in Liberia. To learn more, visit: www.cuac.org

The Rev. Adrian Cardenas-Torres is a deacon serving as clergy-in-charge of the Cathedral of Saint Luke in the Republic of Panama and a member of the Civil Society Network of the United Nations

Department of Economic & Social Affairs addressing women's rights. Since 2008, he has been a consultant to the United Nations Population Fund (UNFPA), contributing to the creation of national and regional platforms and networks of faith-based organizations in America, Europe, and Asia as well as tackling the challenges of gender-based violence and sexual and reproductive health and rights. Prior to this, he served as the diploma program coordinator of the Anglican International Center for Theological Studies in the Episcopal Diocese of Venezuela. He has exhibited a passion for nearly twenty years for social action from the civil society basis (NGOs and faith-based organizations) doing partnership with the United Nations and as UNFPA's consultant in the making and publishing of materials on women's rights in the fields of gender-based violence and sexual and reproductive health. To learn more, visit: http://csonet.org

The Rev. Canon Brother Andrew A.L. de Carpentier is executive director of the Holy Land Institute for Deaf and Deafblind Children in Salt, Jordan. Born in Holland, he is an Anglican monk and ordained priest and a canon of St. George's Cathedral in Jerusalem. He studied civil engineering, special education, and theology and has lived in the Middle East since 1970. Over the years, he has developed extensive first-hand experience in the area of hearing impairment and is recognized by a number of national, regional, and international agencies as an authority and resource person in the fields of sensory impairment and hearing aids, sign language, and special education. He is a founding member and current chair of WWHearing (Worldwide Hearing Care for Developing Countries and Deserving Communities). His goal is for hard-of-hearing, deaf, and deafblind people to participate in family and civic society in a meaningful way and to enable them to make their unique and God-given contribution to an inclusive society. The Arab church's ministry to and with persons with disabilities displaced by war reflects the realization that even Jesus was a refugee. To learn more, visit: www.holyland-deaf.org

The Rt. Rev. Maria Griselda Delgado del Carpio is the bishop of the Episcopal Church of Cuba. She worked closely with Bishop Miguel Tamayo of the Anglican Church of Uruguay, while he served as Cuba's interim bishop. Upon his retirement, Delgado became Cuba's diocesan bishop and is the first woman to serve in that role. Born in Bolivia and formerly the rector of Santa Maria Virgen in Itabo, Cuba, Maria was appointed as bishop coadjutor by the Metropolitan Council of Cuba, which governs the Cuban church in matters of faith and order. The council has overseen the church in Cuba since it separated from the the Episcopal Church in 1967. The Cuban church includes about forty congregations and some 10,000 Episcopalians.

The Rev. G. David Cesar is a priest in the Episcopal Diocese of Haiti. Since 1996, he has served as the director of Ecole de Musique Sainte Trinite, which was founded in 1956. The school has 1,500 students and about fifty-five faculty. He is also the acting conductor of the Holy Trinity Philharmonic Orchestra in Haiti. He has served as rector of St. James Episcopal Church and a member of the clerical staff at Holy Trinity Cathedral. He earned a doctorate in the arts from Universite Royale in Haiti and a doctorate in divinity from Yale University. Cesar is also a violin and viola teacher. He has incorporated music as a means of addressing social justice and poverty. To learn more, visit: www.saintetrinitemusique.wixsite.com/saintetrinitemusique

Jenny Te Paa Daniel has been a pioneer among Indigenous women, becoming the first Maori in the world to gain an academic degree in theology (University of Auckland in 1992) and the first Indigenous

Anglican lay woman to lead an Anglican theological college in the Anglican Communion, serving as principal of Te Rau Kahikatea at St. John's Theological College in Auckland for 22 years. She has served and led a number of international delegations and commissions for the Anglican Communion and the World Council of Churches, including the international Anglican Peace and Justice Network. She has worked to advance women's leadership, in the church and society, including mentoring young women from the third world and indigenous communities. She is one of the most influential women in the Anglican Communion and offers a distinctive voice to Anglican theological reflection. She encourages readers to learn more about Sabeel, which is a globally renowned grassroots organization passionately committed to social justice in the Holy Land. To learn more, visit: www.sabeel.org

The Rev. Stephen Davenport is a retired priest in the Diocese of Washington. He studied at Washington and Lee University, Virginia Theological Seminary, and Yale Divinity School. He has served as parish priest, campus minister, assistant head of school and chaplain, teacher of religion, and American football and soccer coach in the Episcopal dioceses of Kentucky and Washington, D.C. He was the first white assistant to an Eskimo priest in Point Hope, Alaska, participated in a clergy family exchange with the Diocese of Guatemala, and worked in parish partnership programs with an Episcopal church in the Anacostia neighborhood of Washington, D.C. He also worked with the Mountains and Deserts Ministry consisting of parish representatives of Shoshone, Ute, Paiute, and Arrapaho tribes. He has been affiliated with the Holy Trinity Music School, Port-au-Prince, Haiti, since 1970 and received an honorary degree with the Rev. David Cesar in 2013. He has incorporated music as a means of addressing social justice and poverty. To learn more, visit: www.saintetrinitemusique.wixsite.com/saintetrinitemusique

The Most Rev. Glenn N. Davies serves as archbishop of Sydney in the Anglican Church of Australia. Ordained deacon and priest in 1981, he served for two years as an assistant priest in a Sydney parish. In 1983, he was invited to join the faculty of Moore Theological College, Sydney, where he taught Old and New Testament subjects and also served as registrar for most of the thirteen years he was at the college. Beginning in 1995, he served as rector of St. Luke's, Miranda, a Sydney parish, before being consecrated bishop of North Sydney in 2001 and subsequently elected archbishop of Sydney in 2013. He is a strong supporter of Anglican Aid, a not-for-profit Christian organization committed to excellence in the provision of Christian aid to vulnerable communities throughout the world. To learn more, visit: www.anglicanaid.org.au

The Rev. Judy Fentress-Williams is professor of Old Testament at Virginia Theological Seminary. She is an outstanding preacher and also serves on the ministerial staff at the Alfred Street Baptist Church in Alexandria, Virginia. She earned her bachelor's degree in English from Princeton University and received her doctorate in Hebrew Bible from Yale University in 1999. Prior to her appointment at Virginia Seminary, she was a member of the faculty of Hartford Seminary as professor of Hebrew Bible and was also the director of the Black Ministries Program, a program designed to meet the needs of African-American clergy and laity in the greater Hartford area. Fentress-Williams has published numerous essays and has recently published a commentary on the book of Ruth for the *Abingdon Old Testament Commentary Series*. She serves on the Advisory Board for the Office of Religious Life at Princeton University. To learn more, visit: http://www.hartsem.edu/academics/leadership-certificates/black-ministries-program/

The Rev. A. Katherine Grieb is a professor of New Testament at the Virginia Theological Seminary. Archbishop of Canterbury Justin Welby selected her as one of seven preachers chosen from the 80-million-member Anglican Communion to preach at least once each year at Canterbury Cathedral. She is the author of *The Story of Romans: A Narrative Defense of God's Righteousness.* She is a member of the associated clergy team of St. Stephen and the Incarnation/ San Esteban y la Encarnacion Episcopal Church in Washington, D.C. To learn more, visit: www.saintstephensdc.org

David E. Griffith is the executive director of Episcopal Community Services of Philadelphia, a faith-based social service agency committed to providing services that challenge poverty every day. He is the first non-clergy, non-social worker to lead this 145-year-old agency. He comes to this work after forty years as an executive in the for-profit world and is a lifelong Episcopalian. He is married to Jacqui, and they have two adult children, one dog, and a very old cat. To learn more, visit: http://ecsphilly.org/

Bishop Frank T. Griswold served as the XXV Presiding Bishop of the Episcopal Church. He is the author of *Going Home: An Invitation to Jubilee* and *Praying our Days: A Guide and Companion.* He continues a ministry of teaching, conducting conferences and leading retreats. He also serves as bishop visitor of the Society of St. John the Evangelist.

John E. Harris Jr. is the managing partner of LifePlan Partners LLC and a lay leader in the Diocese of Southern Ohio. His involvement in and attraction to the Episcopal Church began in the 1960s during the height of the Civil Rights Movement. It continued during the 1970s when the Diocese of Southern Ohio initiated the Institutional Racism Project that led to his serving in many leadership capacities, including an eighteen-year term as treasurer of the Episcopal Community Service Foundation and most recently a seven-year term as treasurer of the diocese. He is the immediate past president of the Union of Black Episcopalians. To learn more, visit: www.ube.org

Mary M. Higbee has served as an Episcopal volunteer missionary under the direction of mission personnel of the Episcopal Church. Her mission work took her to South Sudan to open a secondary school and to Kenya to do teacher training workshops. She is currently active in her parish, working with adult formation groups, and holds a national office in the Society of Companions of the Holy Cross. To learn more, visit: http://www.episcopalchurch.org/blog/MissionPersonnel

The Rev. Canon Angela S. Ifill is missioner for the Office of Black Ministries for the Episcopal Church, working with black communities of faith—clergy, lay, youth, and young adults—to become centers for mission. This work is accomplished through the New Visions Initiative for Congregational Renewal and Vitality and the RISE initiative, which is a rite of passage for young people. These ministries include intensive and intentional work on the part of those involved as they share their faith journeys with one another and share God's love with young people through interactions to build life skills and raise awareness of God-given potential for success. To learn more, visit: http://www.episcopalchurch.org/files/rise_rising_stars_experience.pdf

David Kasievich is the head of school at St. James Episcopal School in Philadelphia. He is a community leader and an advocate for equal access to education. He began his career in education as a high school teacher at several faith-based schools in urban and suburban Philadelphia and Camden, New Jersey. He later served as the executive director for Lasallian Volunteers in Washington, D.C., a program that provides high-quality volunteer teachers to under-resourced cities throughout the United States and Mexico. Kasievich returned to Philadelphia to serve as the director of development at two urban schools in Philadelphia. Together with partners Audrey Evans and the Rev. Sean Mullen, he cofounded St. James School in 2011. It is an Episcopal middle school located in Philadelphia's underserved Allegheny West neighborhood. The St. James' School is committed to educating traditionally under-resourced students from the neighborhood in a nurturing environment and providing students and their families with the tools and support necessary to thrive and excel. St. James School is breaking the cycle of poverty through education. To learn more, visit: www.stjamesphila.org

The Rev. Canon Vicentia Kgabe is the dean of the College of the Transfiguration (the provincial seminary) in Grahamstown, South Africa. She is passionate about theological education and issues of social justice. Ordained a priest in 2003, she has served in several parishes around the Diocese of Johannesburg and as rector of the Parish of Weltevreden St. Michael and All Angels. She was an archdeacon in the Diocese of Johannesburg, where she had responsibility for the promotion and discernment of vocations to the ordained ministry of the church. In 2014 she was appointed rector of the College of the Transfiguration. To learn more, visit: http://www.cott.co.za/

The Rev. Mike Kinman is rector of All Saints' Episcopal Church in Pasadena, California. He is a disciple of Jesus, husband, father, and rector. He received his bachelor of journalism degree from the University of Missouri and worked as a sportswriter before being called to the priesthood. He studied at Berkeley Divinity School at Yale University and was the 2008 recipient of the John Hines Preaching Award from Virginia Theological Seminary. He previously served as Dean of Christ Church Cathedral in St. Louis, where he was active in the Ferguson uprising after the killing of Michael Brown, and he continues actively to support the young leadership of the movement for black lives across the country. He is also the founding board president of Magdalene St. Louis, a two-year residential program for women who have survived prostitution, violence, and drug abuse. He urges readers to look at Campaign Zero, an organization begun by activists Brittany Packnett, Netta Elzie and DeRay McKesson who met on the streets of Ferguson. It promotes concrete, actionable proposals to end police violence in America. To learn more, visit: www.joincampaignzero.org

The Rev. Canon Robert V. Lee III is a humanitarian, Episcopal priest, and chairman and chief executive officer of Jacksonville, Florida-based nonprofit FreshMinistries and its international arm, Be The Change International. Lee is responsible for the creation of a number of unique and successful global initiatives and partnerships addressing issues of poverty worldwide. Efforts began with programs vital to the restoration of core-city Jacksonville and continued with partnerships in Africa designed to combat HIV/AIDS and to address the United Nation's Millennium Development Goals. Founded in 1989, FreshMinistries focuses on sustainable outreach in core-city Jacksonville and throughout the world through programs to teach financial literacy, life skills, job preparation, business incubation, and other initiatives aimed at enhancing quality of life in impoverished and crime-ridden neighborhoods. To learn more, visit: www.Freshministries.org

The Rt. Rev. Mark MacDonald is the national Indigenous Anglican bishop in Canada and the North American president for the World Council of Churches. He served as the bishop of Alaska from 1997-2007. The Anglican Council of Indigenous Peoples is devoted to indigenous rights and self-determination. To learn more, visit: www.anglican.ca/about/ccc/acip/

Canon Delene Mark is the chief executive officer of HOPE Africa, a social development program of the Anglican Church of Southern Africa. Delene lives in Cape Town and is a lay canon in the Anglican Church. She holds degrees in music, social development and policy, and management. To learn more, visit: http://www.hopeafricausa.org/

Dr. H.M. McFarling III is president of Atlanta Obstetrics and Gynecology Associates and has been with the practice since 1984. McFarling trained at Emory University and is board certified in obstetrics and gynecology. He is the chairman of Piedmont Healthcare in Atlanta, Georgia and is the vice president of Atlanta Women's Healthcare Specialists, LLC. While in training at Emory University Medical School and residency at Grady Memorial Hospital in Atlanta, McFarling discovered St. Luke's Episcopal Parish, where he married his wife, Ginna, and they raised their three daughters Kelly, Erin, and Allie. He has served in national leadership roles with the Consortium of Endowed Episcopal Parishes, the Episcopal Church Foundation, and CREDO and helped to start Genesis Shelter, a safe place for homeless women with newborns. To learn more, visit: http://ourhousega.org/

Sara Miles is the author of *Take this Bread, Jesus Freak, City of God,* and other books. She is the founder and director of The Food Pantry at St. Gregory of Nyssa Episcopal Church in San Francisco, which gives away free fresh groceries to hundreds of people every week. To learn more, visit: www.thefoodpantry.org

Esther M. Mombo is a lecturer in church history, theologies from women's perspectives, and interfaith courses at St. Paul's University in Limuru, Kenya, where she also serves as the director of International Partnerships. Mombo has served on numerous church boards and has consulted globally on issues regarding women and ministry and theological education. Mombo has previously served as the deputy vice chancellor of academics at St. Paul's University. She is a member of the Circle of Concerned African Woman Theologians and writes on issues such as HIV/AIDS, Christian-Muslim relations and poverty in Africa. She works closely with Program for Christian and Muslim Relations in Africa. Mombo studied at St. Paul's University in Kenya, Trinity College in Dublin, and received her doctorate from Edinburgh University in Scotland. She encourages readers to learn more about the Cornerstone Preparatory Academy, a ministry that provides spiritual and physical support and emotional healing to children in Kenya. To learn more, visit: www.naomisvillage.org

The Ven. Dr. Pamela M. Nesbit is a retired clinical psychologist. She has served as a deacon for twenty years and is the archdeacon responsible for the formation, deployment, and pastoral care of deacons in the Episcopal Diocese of Pennsylvania. She also serves as deacon at the Philadelphia Episcopal Cathedral, which has a weekly food distribution program called Cathedral Table. Every Monday people come from the surrounding neighborhoods to receive meat, canned goods, and other nourishing items. Recipients are not required to demonstrate need. All are welcome. Those who desire may also receive the eucharist and the laying on of hands. To learn more, visit: www.philadelphiacathedral.org

Will O'Brien is founder and coordinator of The Alternative Seminary, a grassroots program of biblical and theological study in Philadelphia. For over thirty-five years, he has been involved in advocacy on issues of homelessness and poverty, including working at Project HOME. He has done extensive writing and teaching on issues of biblical discipleship in the modern world. To learn more, visit: www.projecthome.org

The Rev. Nurya Love Parish is co-founder and executive director of Plainsong Farm and Ministry, a farm-based ministry in greater Grand Rapids, Michigan. She serves as the Province V representative on the Episcopal Church's Advisory Council for the Stewardship of Creation and edits Grow Christians (www.growchristians.org), an online community for disciples practicing faith at home, sponsored by Forward Movement. Plainsong Farm and Ministry (www.plainsongfarm.com) grows food for people and people for God. Along with their local charitable food ministry, the farm also works at the intersection of Christian faith and sustainable agriculture through connecting the dots of the Christian food movement. To learn more, visit: www.christianfoodmovement.org

Sonia H. Patterson has served as president and chief executive officer of Five Talents, USA since 2012. She is passionately committed to international development programs that make a lasting difference in people's lives. She first observed the power of small business development to fight poverty as a Peace Corps volunteer in Honduras. Since that time, she has pioneered businesses and nonprofit programs in the United States, Latin America, the Middle East, Africa, and Asia, working and traveling in over seventy countries. She has twenty years of entrepreneurial experience in developing business, non-governmental, and community relations. Fluent in English and Spanish, she holds a a bachelor's degree from Wittenberg University and an MBA from Thunderbird School of Global Management, where she concentrated on global entrepreneurship. Seventy-nine percent of those reached by Five Talents are women, who are often marginalized in their cultures. Five Talents works to instill and restore dignity in those who want to lift themselves and their families out of poverty through literacy, innovative savings and financial-inclusion programs, biblical-based business training, and spiritual development. To learn more, visit: www.fivetalents.org

The Rev. Nicholas T. Porter is an Episcopal priest and the co-founder and executive director of Jerusalem Peacebuilders, Inc., an interfaith, nonprofit organization working to empower tomorrow's peacebuilders in Israel and Palestine. A longtime resident of Europe and the Middle East, Nicholas now lives with his wife and their three daughters in Vermont. Jerusalem Peacebuilders promotes transformational encounters among the peoples of Jerusalem and the wider Middle East. In partnership with local organizations, it specializes in experiential learning programs that provide youth and adults with the skills, support and confidence to advance peacebuilding, interfaith citizenship, and social change. To learn more, visit: www.jerusalempeacebuilders.org

Robert W. Radtke is president of Episcopal Relief and Development, where he is deeply engaged in the work of alleviating hunger and improving the food supply, creating economic opportunities and strengthening communities, promoting health and fighting disease, and responding to disasters and rebuilding communities. To learn more, visit www.episcopalrelief.org

The Rev. Lee Anne Reat serves as the vicar of St. John's Episcopal Church, an inner-city, primarily Appalachian, mission church, in Columbus, Ohio. Two services are held weekly—a traditional indoor service and Street Church, which celebrates Holy Eucharist in a vacant lot at a busy intersection. Other ministries include a weekly community meal, Confluence (a young adult Episcopal Service Corps program), an outdoor learning garden for local schools, and more. To learn more, visit: www.st-johns-columbus.org

The Rev. Austin K. Rios is the rector of St. Paul's Within the Walls Episcopal Church in Rome, Italy, and director of the Joel Nafuma Refugee Center (JNRC) in the heart of Rome. The center welcomes over two hundred guests each weekday, including many refugees who come from Mali and Afghanistan. The services offered in the center range from basic assistance to settlement services and seek to address the needs of the whole person. Before moving to Rome, Rios served for seven years in the Diocese of Western North Carolina as a curate and then as diocesan canon for Spanish-speaking ministries and vicar of La Capilla de Santa Maria, Hendersonville. Much of his ministry involved advocacy on behalf of undocumented persons and connecting English and Spanish-speaking Episcopalians across the traditional divides of language, class, and culture. Since coming to Rome, Rios has represented the Episcopal Church in ecumenical and Anglican Communion events while continuing to look for ways to expand the JNRC's programs and offerings for refugees. To learn more, visit: www.jnrc.it

Sister Mary Scullion has been involved in service work and advocacy for homeless and mentally ill persons since 1978. She is co-founder and executive director of Project HOME, a nationally recognized nonprofit in Philadelphia. She has received numerous awards for her work, including being named one of TIME Magazine's "World's Most Influential People" in 2009. She is a member of the Sisters of Mercy religious order. To learn more, visit: www.projecthome.org

The Rev. Edmund K. "Ned" Sherrill II is head of school at Church Farm School in Exton, Pennsylvania. He became the fourth head of school in 2009. He is an ordained Episcopal priest, who received his bachelor's degree from Macalester College and his master's of divinity from Yale Divinity School. Prior to becoming head of the Church

Farm School, he served as head chaplain and director of the religion department at St. Mark's School in Southborough, Massachusetts. He has also served at St. John's Church and School, Guam, Micronesia; St. Paul's School in Concord, New Hampshire; and Wooster School in Danbury, Connecticut. The Church Farm School was founded in 1918 and focused on instilling its students with character according to three clear tenets: the value of religion, the value of hard work, and the value of education. Church Farm School opened its doors to the families of boys who may not have been otherwise able to afford such an opportunity. Today, the school is a boarding/day college preparatory school for boys of all backgrounds in grades 8-12. It utilizes a sliding scale tuition model and uniquely offers a residential, college prep education to boys living on or near the social/economic margins. To learn more, visit: www.gocfs.net

The Rev. Richard L. Tolliver is the rector of St. Edmund's Episcopal Church and president and chief executive officer of St. Edmund's Redevelopment Corporation in Chicago, Illinois. He has served parishes in New York City, Boston, Washington, D.C., and Chicago. He is a former associate country director of the United States Peace Corps in Kenya and country director in Mauritania. He has served on numerous church, civic, and corporate boards. Tolliver founded St. Edmund's Redevelopment Corporation (SERC) in 1990 as a nonprofit community development corporation devoted to revitalizing the housing stock of Chicago's Washington Park neighborhood. The organization has constructed or renovated over 700 units of housing located in thirty-one buildings at a cost of $104 million. To learn more, visit: www.stedmundsrc.org

The Rev. Winnie Varghese serves as director of justice and reconciliation at historic Trinity Episcopal Church, Wall Street in New York City. She is a popular blogger on the Huffington Post and respected for her work as rector of St. Mark's in the Bowery, a diverse, progressive church in New York. She leads social action efforts at national and local levels and has served as a key leader in the Executive Council and House of Deputies of the Episcopal Church. She is author of *Church Meets World: Church's Teachings for a Changing World, Volume 4.* To learn more, visit: https://www.trinitywallstreet.org/

Br. David Vryhof, SSJE, is a priest and brother of the Society of Saint John the Evangelist, a religious order for men in the Episcopal Church (www.ssje.org). He is an experienced preacher, teacher, retreat leader, and spiritual director. Br. David currently serves as the novice guardian for the Society, overseeing the formation of new members entering the community. He was a teacher of the deaf before entering monastic life, and he continues to be involved in ministry with deaf people, including helping SSJE work with the Episcopal Conference of the Deaf. Deaf and hard-of-hearing people are often marginalized and isolated in society and in the church because of the challenges they face in communicating with others. To learn more, visit: www.ecdeaf.org.

The Rev. Hillary T. West is an ordained priest with a passion for parish ministry, mission, and service. She serves as the rector of Epiphany Episcopal Church in Oak Hill, Virginia. She has served with St. James's, Richmond as a Christian educator. Following ordination, she served with Christ Church, Richmond, and St. Thomas' Church, Whitemarsh, in Fort Washington, Pennsylvania before coming to Northern Virginia. She encourages readers to learn more about the Hope and Resurrection Secondary School in South Sudan, which is changing lives and bringing peace and hope in a war-torn region. To learn more, visit: http://www.hopeforhumanityinc.org

The Rev. Marek P. Zabriskie is the rector of St. Thomas' Episcopal Church in Fort Washington, Pennsylvania. He is also the founder of The Bible Challenge and the founder and director of the Center for Biblical Studies, which promotes and shares The Bible Challenge across the United States and around the world. Since its founding in 2011, more than 500,000 people have participated in The Bible Challenge in over 2,500 churches in more than 50 countries. He has edited six books for Forward Movement relating to The Bible Challenge and wrote *Doing the Bible Better: The Bible Challenge and the Transformation of the Episcopal Church* with Church Publishing. He has served churches in Nashville, Tennessee, and Richmond, Virginia, prior to moving to Pennsylvania. To learn more, visit: www.thecenterforbiblicalstudies.org

About Forward Movement

Forward Movement is committed to inspiring disciples and empowering evangelists. While we produce great resources like this book, Forward Movement is not a publishing company. We are a ministry.

Our mission is to support you in your spiritual journey, to help you grow as a follower of Jesus Christ. Publishing books, daily reflections, studies for small groups, and online resources is an important way that we live out this ministry. More than a half million people read our daily devotions through *Forward Day by Day*, which is also available in Spanish (*Adelante Día a Día*) and Braille, online, as a podcast, and as an app for your smartphones or tablets. It is mailed to more than fifty countries, and we donate nearly 30,000 copies each quarter to prisons, hospitals, and nursing homes. We actively seek partners across the Church and look for ways to provide resources that inspire and challenge.

A ministry of The Episcopal Church for eighty years, Forward Movement is a nonprofit organization funded by sales of resources and gifts from generous donors. To learn more about Forward Movement and our resources, please visit us at www.forwardmovement.org (or www.venadelante.org).

We are delighted to be doing this work and invite your prayers and support.